The Gingerbread Inn

or

A Christmas Adventure

For Haley with love —

by

Betty Stewart Behringer

Betty Stewart Behringer

To Jason Parker and all the
other boys and girls of
Trinity School.

ISBN 0-932616-26-7

Library of Congress Catalog Card No. 92-081047

THE GINGERBREAD INN

As they rose to their feet, the hood slipped back off Klutter's head.

Chapter 1
The Gingerbread Inn

"AMY, I DO BELIEVE WE'RE LOST!" exclaimed Peter as he slowly turned around so that he could see in every direction. Actually, all he could see were heavy underbrush and trees.

"Let's holler for Mother and Daddy just as loud as we can," suggested his younger sister. "Maybe they'll hear us and come."

"All right. One-two-three-go!"

Together, they called as loudly as they could: "Mother! Daddy! M-O-T-H-E-R! D-A-A-D-E-E! Mother! Daddy!"

They waited for a reply, but there was no sound except for the biting December wind as it swept through the oaks and pines and rattled the leaves of the holly trees. Once again they called. They tried a third and a fourth time; but there was no response. Tears filled Amy's eyes.

"Now don't do that!" warned her brother, "or your tears may freeze into icicles — and then won't you look funny?"

"I don't care! We shouldn't have walked so far away. I want Mother and Daddy!"

"Oh, don't act like a baby, Amy. Come on, now. We'll find them. All we have to do is just keep walking. Even if we don't get back to them, we're bound to come out to a road. Then we'll hail a car and tell the driver we're lost and he'll help us. He'll take us to a telephone. Maybe he'll take us home. Now stop crying and come on."

Amy sniffled and rubbed her sleeve across her face.

"My hands are cold, Peter."

"Well, put them in your pockets."

"My feet are cold, too."

"Well, come on, let's walk."

5

They made their way through the trees and thick underbrush as best they could without a path. At last they came to a hill that rose steeply before them.

"If we climb to the top of this hill," said Peter, "maybe we'll be able to see a road or a house — or even a trail."

Holding hands, the children clambered up the slope. The ground was thickly carpeted with pine needles, and more than once they nearly lost their footing. At last they reached the top and looked about them. Before them the hill sloped downward even more sharply. Search as they might in every direction, they could see no sign of a path or road. Suddenly, as they were wondering what to do next, Amy's feet slid out from under her, and she began to slide down the slope before them as if she were on a very slippery sliding board.

"Wait! Wait!" cried Peter as he ran after his sister.

"I can't stop! Peter! Help!"

Then Peter tripped over the root of a giant oak and fell flat on his face. He, too, began to slide. Faster and faster he flew. He tried to grab hold of a branch or bush, but he found that he couldn't hang on to anything. Everything in the forest had suddenly become as slippery as ice. A low branch struck him in the face, just missing his left eye. He decided that there was no use struggling. Closing his eyes tightly, he slid onward pell mell. The hill appeared to grow longer and longer. He opened his eyes a crack to see before him the opening of a huge, dark cave.

"Good grief! There're probably bears in there!" he gasped. But before he could take another breath, he swooped in. Closing his eyes tightly and gritting his teeth, he awaited disaster. Then suddenly he struck something soft and cold. He had stopped at last.

Slowly Peter opened his eyes. He was sitting in a gigantic snowdrift, and there were Amy's feet only a few yards away. He jumped and pulled her out of the snow.

"*Now* where are we?" she gasped, after she had brushed the snow from her hair and clothes and recovered a little of her breath.

Peter looked around. The forest had changed in appearance. There were still the oaks, beeches, maples, pines, and hollies; but the trees here appeared much older and very much bigger, with gnarled roots and low, overhanging limbs. There was very little undergrowth, the ground being clear, open, and relatively even and flat. But the most surprising change was in the weather. Here everything was covered with snow. Every leaf on each holly tree was like a tiny saucer holding a little spoonful of snow while the green edges of the leaf rimmed the white, and the red holly berries glistened and shone like tiny Christmas balls. The branches of the trees and the pine needles were coated with ice and they sparkled and danced in the bright winter sunshine.

"Wherever we are, it's beautiful!" exclaimed Peter.

"But how are we ever to find our way home now?" wailed Amy.

"Come on, now, don't cry. Look at this. This looks like a path — here between these trees. Let's walk along it. Maybe it will take us to a highway."

He took her by the hand and the two children trudged along through the snow among the great trees of the strange but beautiful woodland.

They had not walked more than half a mile when Amy stopped.

"I smell something," she said.

"Me, too," agreed Peter.

"It smells good!"

"It smells *delicious!*"

Suddenly the children remembered that they hadn't eaten anything since breakfast. They had wandered off to gather firewood while their parents were preparing the picnic lunch and building a campfire, so they had eaten no lunch. Now the sun, which was moving closer and closer to the horizon, told them plainly that it was late afternoon.

They began to trot briskly along the path. The delectable, spicy aroma grew stronger, until suddenly they emerged from the woods and saw before them a low valley. In the clearing there stood a brown house with a steeply pitched roof that was entirely covered by snow. Icicles of all sizes hung from the eves. The rays of the setting sun danced through them and bounced off and transformed them into pointed cylinders of diamonds. Candlelight

7

flickered through the windowpanes. Smoke was rising from the chimney in a straight column. It was the spicy aroma of the smoke that the children had smelled.

"Look!" cried Amy, pointing to the house.

"Now we're all right," Peter reassured her. Yet as they approached the building, he began to feel waves of apprehension. This house did not resemble any other house that he had ever seen. Come to think of it, the forest looked different, too — not at all like Chester Woods where he and Amy and their parents went frequently for hikes and picnics. Even the snow seemed different, somehow. Everything was more beautiful. However, since the snow was perishingly cold, they hastened their steps toward the cottage.

As they approached, the oaken door opened with a creaking sound. A little old white-haired lady in a green dress and red hood and shawl stood in the doorway. She smiled kindly and nodded to the children.

"Hello!" she called, and a tinkling echo like tiny icicles blown by the wind accompanied her words. "I saw you coming. Whatever are you doing here, alone in the Great Forest, when a blizzard is about to sweep in?"

"We're lost," said Peter. "We can't find our way back to our parents. Can you help us?"

"Come in, my dears, come in. Welcome to Gingerbread Inn. As for finding your parents, I don't know that I can help you. But you mustn't stand out there in the cold. Come in and warm yourselves. I've just baked a fresh batch of gingerbread cookies. You shall have all that you want with baked apples and cream and warm, soft beds for the night. Tomorrow we shall see what can be done about finding your family. Come, come now," she insisted. "Already the North Wind is sweeping down upon us with his icy breath and snow, which he will scatter over the entire land during the night."

Indeed, Peter and Amy needed no further inducement. They crossed the lighted threshold and found themselves in a warm, spacious room containing half a dozen round tables with chairs. At the far end there was an enormous hearth. A black and white cat lay curled up on a green velvet cushion by the fireside. Blazing birch logs crackled invitingly, and Grandmother Hollyberry — for that was the old lady's name — led the children to the fire to warm them after their chilling walk through the snow-clad woods.

Soon she had set up places for them at one of the tables, and the girl and boy were devouring fresh, sweet milk, spicy gingerbread, and rosy baked apples in saucers of rich, golden cream.

"Now you must each drink a cup of elflower tea to warm you well, and then off to bed with you both."

"Mother *never* lets us drink tea," objected Amy.

"This tea is different from your mother's tea," explained Grandmother. "It is made from dried elflower leaves, the milk of milkweed, water from the Crystal Brook, and sugar from the Merry Maples. It will make you strong and wise and will give you happy dreams tonight."

"Then I guess Mother wouldn't mind," replied Amy.

Grandmother Hollyberry had already poured two steaming mugs of elflower tea and set them before the children. The marvelous fragrance invited a taste. Peter sipped some noisily.

"Good!" he exclaimed. Then Amy tried hers.

"Yummy!" she agreed, and before she had quite emptied her mug, she dropped off to sleep in her chair. Grandmother Hollyberry put her finger on her lips to make Peter be silent. Then picking Amy up in her arms, she nodded to him to follow. They crossed the room to a narrow staircase and mounted the creaking steps to the floor above. There were several bedrooms upstairs. They entered one. Grandmother laid Amy gently into a soft, old-fashioned feather bed and covered her with an eiderdown quilt. She silently pointed to Peter's bed in the opposite corner.

"I'll leave the candle in the window for a night light so you needn't be afraid of the dark," she whispered. "Now good night and sleep tight and never mind Sir North Wind and his storm."

"Good night, Grandmother," whispered Peter, " — and thank you. Thank you very much."

Grandmother Hollyberry nodded and smiled, and suddenly the room seemed to glow with a brilliant light. Grandmother

Hollyberry's white hair flickered with gold and her face flushed with youth and beauty. Peter blinked in astonishment. In that tiny second, when he opened his eyes again, the room was as dimly lit as before. Grandmother Hollyberry was just as old and gray as ever as she tiptoed through the doorway and softly closed the door behind her.

"Great jumping beans!" exclaimed Peter. He whistled softly through the space between his front teeth. "Wow! Wait till Mom and Dad hear about *this*!" But before he could think any more about it, he, too, had dropped off into a deep, restful sleep.

Chapter 2

The Night Visitors

S IR NORTH WIND HOWLED AND DROVE through the Great Forest. He snow-blasted every tree and bush and every foot of the land. When he reached the Gingerbread Inn, he roared up to it and blew his mightiest, but he succeeded only in dislodging a few bricks from the rim of the chimney and loosening a shutter. He took great satisfaction from his mischievous accomplishment and proceeded to slam the shutter back and forth, making a loud and irritating clatter, until he finally broke out a small pane from one of the attic windows. Seeing that he could do no further harm, he soon wearied of the sport and moved on to find a more likely object to wreck.

The children slept soundly through the storm. They didn't hear the loud knocking on the Inn door late that night, as two more wayfarers arrived and requested food and lodging for the night. Grandmother Hollyberry let them in. The strangers were heavily wrapped in hoods and cloaks. They stomped the snow from their high boots as they entered.

Without removing their outer garments, they sat themselves down by the fire and ate the steaming, delicious stew that Grandmother placed before them. Long after she had turned in for the night, the two hooded figures continued to sit by the fire, drinking huge tankards of ale as they talked softly to one another.

Sometime later Peter awoke from his deep sleep. He lay in bed for a few moments wondering where he was. As he looked around the room, still dimly lit by the single candle in the window, the events of the preceding day gradually returned to his mind. Amy was sound asleep; but sleep was no longer in Peter's eyes.

He climbed out of bed and tiptoed to the window. The room was very cold. Scraping the frost from a pane with the blade of his penknife, he peeped out into the night. The storm had passed,

11

leaving great drifts of snow upon the ground. The boughs of the pines were weighted heavily and sagging under their load of snow. A full moon was playing peek-a-boo with some of Sir North Wind's skittering cloud wraiths. Perhaps it was all because of the spicy gingerbread he had eaten, but suddenly Peter felt very, very thirsty.

"I'll just sneak down the steps to the kitchen and get a drink of water," decided Peter. Very softly, so as not to disturb anyone, he opened the door and slipped out into the dark hallway. Firelight and candlelight from below lit up the stairway, and he tiptoed softly to the top landing. Peeking down through the banister, he saw the two guests as they sat and talked by the hearth. There was something about the mysterious, hooded figures that made him hesitate to go down. As he crouched on the top step and watched them, he could hear snatches of their conversation.

"It is a great plan, Klatter, but it will never work. How can we possibly kidnap him? There are too many dwarfs about. They will defend him."

"Ah, Klutter! You have apparently not heard about the secret weapon!"

"What sort of secret weapon?"

"The secret weapon that is being finished right now. The Black Widows have been spinning it for twenty years," replied Klatter.

The strangers' voices subsided to a whisper, and although Peter strained his ears, he could catch only a word or two of the conversation. Finally they raised their voices a little and he heard the one addressed as Klutter ask.

"Why are they giving this thing to us?"

The other laughed.

"They are 'giving' it to us for seven bags of our most precious gems — our largest and finest rubies, emeralds, sapphires, and diamonds!"

"Horrors, Klatter! That's a terrible price — even for so great a weapon! What does the Council say?"

"The Council has fully approved the purchase. It is to be delivered to his Royal Highness tomorrow in exchange for the treasure."

"So! You have accomplished much since I have been guarding the Golden Horn."

"Hush!" whispered Klatter, as he looked around. "Do not even mention *that!* If any of them learn that we have the Horn and where it is hidden, we would all be undone!"

"Yes, you're right. As long as we have *that,* we're safe." He looked toward the stairway. Peter drew back into the darkness of the upstairs hall. He scarcely dared to breathe.

"Let's retire for the night," suggested Klatter. "We'll rise early and leave before daybreak. We can't afford to be recognized by Grandmother Hollyberry. We must reach the caves in time for the big ceremony."

As they rose to their feet, the hood slipped back off Klutter's head. Peter saw that Klutter's head was quite huge for his size and covered with thick, coarse hair. But that was not the most surprising thing about him. Klutter had two enormous, hairy ears that stood straight up from his head and tapered into points.

As Klutter and Klatter crossed the room toward the stairway, Peter literally flew back into his bedroom, his heart nearly thumping out of his body. Closing the door as softly as possible in his hurry, he picked up a board that was propped nearby and slipped it through two handles that were fastened to the walls on either side of the door for the purpose of bolting the door securely.

"What was *that?*" he heard Klatter ask, as he paused midway up the stairs.

"Could someone have overheard us?" asked Klutter. "Maybe somebody was hiding in this dark hall."

"Ah! So! Let's try the doors." Someone grasped the doorknob and tried to open the door. "It is barred from within!" Peter heard the hoarse whisper.

"Well, let us be off. Nobody could have heard very much; but if we wake up Grandmother Hollyberry and *she* recognizes us, the gnomes' plans could all be spoiled."

"You are right, Klutter. Besides, I'm very tired. Let's go to bed."

Peter listened as the sounds of their heavy footsteps passed on down the hall and his heart began to beat normally again.

13

"Good grief! Great jumping beans!" Peter whistled softly through his teeth. Needless to say, he did not sleep any more that night. Peter, however, was not the only one who had overheard the plotters.

Little Mistress Mousie, her woven basket on her arm, came tripping to her front door in the wall of the Inn near the fireplace to do her usual nightly food-gathering for her family. Mistress Mousie knew that Grandmother Hollyberry never begrudged her a morsel of cheese and a few crumbs for her hungry wee babies. Even Homer, Grandmother's black and white cat, pretended to be asleep when Mistress Mousie came, although occasionally she would see the glitter of his eyes peeping at her as she went about her tasks. Usually Homer was curled up on his cushion near the fireplace, but tonight, because of the strangers, he had taken refuge atop the high cupboard where the crockery was kept, so that Klutter and Klatter had not even been aware of his presence.

But Homer had kept his pink ears open. He had overheard everything. He watched the gnomes through slitted eyelids until they had disappeared up the stairs. Just as soon as Mistress Mousie emerged from her little doorway, he made a great leap and landed almost upon her.

"Goodness gracious me!" squealed Mistress Mousie, and in her fright she dropped her basket and knocked her hat all askew.

"Never mind all that," said Homer with a great merowr. "There's mischief afoot. More mischief than we can cope with, maybe! But, merowr! We have to try to cope!"

Mistress Mousie adjusted her hat and smoothed out her skirt and picked up her basket.

"Whatever *is* the matter?" she asked nervously. She was always a wee bit nervous when Homer was around, but now she was standing within a paw's reach. She couldn't help seeing his pointed teeth and the tips of his claws as he extended and withdrew them — a kind of nervous twitch he had had since kittenhood.

"There are two gnomes named Klutter and Klatter upstairs. They have been here plotting the worst kind of mischief. If we don't stop them and the others, they will very likely destroy every living creature in the Great Forest. Me-e-rowr!"

14

"Oh dear, oh dear! Whatever are they going to *do*?" wailed Mistress Mousie.

"Listen carefully. I shall tell you everything I have overheard. Then you must get this plot to the Mouse King, for you mice have the best underground organization in the Great Forest — next to the gnomes themselves. They are stronger because they have magic, while we animals have only the gifts of Nature. Perhaps the mice can think of something that will ruin the gnomes' plan."

He then drew even closer to Mistress Mousie's left ear and whispered for a long time until he had told her all that he had managed to hear.

"Oh, dear! Yes, yes! You are certainly a clever cat, Homer. I shall get this information to the Mouse Underground at once. Oh, dear! I hope we're not too late," squeaked Mistress Mousie.

"That's the spirit, my dear! I shall wait here to see if I can pick up any more information. Now hurry off, and don't waste any time."

"Oh, yes! Oh, yes!" And Mistress Mousie, quite forgetting her hungry wee children, scampered off through the hole in the wainscoting and disappeared from sight.

Homer yawned a great yawn and arched his back in a big stretch. Then giving a spring to the back of a chair and another to the top of the cupboard, he curled up into a furry ball to await developments.

Chapter 3
The Golden Horn

PETER LAY ON HIS COT AND WAITED for the sun to rise. Just as the first light began to appear in the East, he heard a door open and close and the sound of heavy footsteps in the hall. He waited breathlessly as they stopped at his door. He heard an exchange of whispers. Then someone tried to open the door, but the bolt was secure. When they found that the door was still fastened from within, Klutter and Klatter descended the stairway. He heard the creak of the heavy oaken door and the sound of it as it closed behind them.

Leaping out of bed, he ran to the window. Klutter and Klatter were walking briskly toward the forest, leaving their trail behind them in the newly fallen snow. The sun was peeping above the horizon through the base of the tree trunks, and both the sky and snow-clad earth glowed with the exquisite rosy colors of a fresh, new day. Peter aroused his sleeping sister.

"Amy, Amy, get up quickly. We must find Grandmother Hollyberry at once!"

"Why?" asked Amy, rubbing the Sleepy Man from her eyes.

"Last night I woke up. I was thirsty, so I was going downstairs for a drink of water when I heard two gnomes plotting to kidnap somebody with some kind of secret weapon."

"What? Two gnomes? Peter, are you crazy? Gnomes aren't real. They're only in fairy tales. You must have been dreaming."

"*These* gnomes are real! Hurry! We haven't any time to lose."

"Oh, all right, all right," replied Amy frowning, as she searched under the bed for her left shoe. "But I still don't believe in gnomes!"

When they had descended the stairs, they found Homer and Grandmother Hollyberry in the warm, cheerful kitchen. She was

16

stirring up a bowl of blueberry pancakes; and when she saw the children, she called to them to come in for breakfast.

"Now, Amy and Peter, we must give some thought as to how we can reunite you with your parents," she began, as they all sat down at the breakfast table.

Peter suddenly realized that he had momentarily forgotten all about that problem.

"They must be dreadfully worried about you both by now," she added.

"Yes," agreed Amy. "Mother worries if we are a few minutes late getting home from school."

Peter cleared his throat.

"We surely do want to get home as soon as possible," he began. "But last night something happened here that I must tell you about."

"Peter had a nightmare," sniffed Amy.

"I did *not!*"

"Well, child, tell us what happened," said Grandmother, leaning forward and eyeing Peter inquisitively.

Thus encouraged, Peter recounted everything that had occurred from the time he awoke until he watched the gnomes trudging away through the snow at sunrise. As he proceeded with his tale, Grandmother's expression became more and more anxious.

"Goodness me!" she exclaimed when Peter had finally finished. "This *is* serious. Klutter and Klatter — those two rascals! Whom could they be after? Did they name *anyone?*"

Peter shook his head.

"Did you say they spoke of dwarfs?"

"Yes."

"Oh, my! Could it be — Oh, that would be terrible! But it makes sense!"

"*What?*" asked both the children together.

"It might be Santa Claus they're after."

"That would be terrible if they kidnapped Santa Claus," cried Amy. "Nobody would get any toys!"

"Santa Claus? Pooh! I don't believe in Santa any more," said Peter scornfully.

17

"Whether or not you believe in someone, my dear, has very little relationship to that individual's state-of-being. Let me assure you, Peter, that Santa and his dwarfs live no farther than twenty-five or thirty miles from here on a high mountain in the deepest part of the Great Forest."

"They *do?*" cried Amy. "Then perhaps we can go see him. Oh, I do want that beautiful doll that has real golden hair I can wash and curl!"

"If the gnomes are actually plotting to destroy Santa," mused Grandmother Hollyberry, "we must warn him at once. He will know what to do."

"Even if there *is* a Santa Claus, why would the gnomes want to hurt him?" asked Peter.

"The gnomes are very strange creatures," she replied. "They spend their entire lives in dark caves underground and in tunnels that they themselves dig. They do nothing but work, work, work — digging for precious metals and gems which they fashion into all sorts of priceless objects. Although they are the wealthiest creatures on earth, since they actually own and control most of the world's treasures, they do not know how to use their riches wisely to bring pleasure and happiness to either themselves or others.

"Because they are extremely selfish, they do nothing but work and hoard their valuables. They rarely venture into the beautiful world above ground, nor do they go picnicking in the Great Forest, nor vacationing anywhere.

"There is something else about them, too. Because they have chosen to work and hoard, they believe that everyone else should do likewise. They believe that it is foolish — even wrong — to give someone something that that person hasn't earned through hard work. To a gnome, the spirit of love and generosity is the true form of evil, and those who give and receive gifts are little better than criminals."

"Wow! Then *that's* why they'd hate Santa Claus," reasoned Peter.

"Exactly, dear Peter," replied Grandmother. "Those gnomes are so confused that, if they *are* able to kidnap Santa and his dwarfs, they will honestly believe they have done a good deed."

18

"Do you mean gnomes think Santa Claus shouldn't bring toys to little children?" inquired Amy.

"The gnomes would like to destroy Christmas altogether. They have formed numerous committees which attempt to influence people everywhere by their underground activities. They say such things as these: 'People who believe in Santa Claus are sick; children will be spoiled by being led to believe they can get something for nothing in life; Christmas is only a modern version of a pagan holiday'; while the trolls, who are the most misguided of all the gnomes, even claim that the Christ child, whose birth we celebrate, never really lived."

"Great jumping beans!" exclaimed Peter.

"I think they must be bad," said Amy.

"Did you tell me everything you overheard? Try to remember — every little detail?"

"Ye-e-s — well, I think so. Well, there was one other thing they mentioned. Something about a golden horn that would ruin their plans if it was ever found."

"The Golden Horn!" cried Grandmother, clasping her hands in excitement. "What did they say about the Golden Horn? Think hard, dear boy."

Peter frowned. "I can't remember anything special. They just mentioned it — let's see — one of them said he'd been somewhere guarding it for a long time."

"Where? Where?" cried Grandmother wringing her hands.

"I don't know. I'm not even sure they said where."

"What's so important about this Golden Horn?" asked Amy.

"Ah! I shall have to tell you the whole story, I see," sighed Grandmother Hollyberry. "But while I tell you, keep trying to recall where he said he has been."

"Okay," said Peter, and the little old lady began:

"I must first explain to you where you are. How you managed to get into the Great Forest, I do not know. There have been others who have come. You and your parents live in another dimension. Somehow you managed to 'slip through'. It will be extremely difficult — maybe impossible — to return you to your proper sphere. It has been accomplished only once in the past. Many,

many generations ago a boy very much like you, Peter, 'slipped through' into our Great Forest. Only the Elf King had magic enough to send him home again. I have heard it said that when he grew up, he became the world's greatest playwright and that he wrote a play about the Great Forest.

"How can we find this Elf King and get back to Mother and Daddy?" asked the practical Peter.

"Alas, child, that may well be impossible because the elves live in still another dimension. Many centuries ago the inhabitants of the Great Forest rescued the son of the Elf King when the trolls had stolen the little prince from his cradle. The Elf King, wishing to show his gratitude, hung a great Golden Horn from a limb of Lothra, the most ancient oak in the Forest.

"Whenever the folk of the Great Forest were threatened with harm, all they had to do was to blow three blasts upon the horn, and the Elves would come to their defense. The magic of the elves is good magic, and therefore the most powerful in all creation. To them is given the power to right all wrongs and correct undeserved misfortunes. They alone have the power to move from one dimension to another.

"As long as the Golden Horn hung by its golden chain from the limb of Lothra, all was well in the Great Forest. However, one night after a violent storm spawned by the North Wind, the limb of Lothra was broken and the Horn disappeared mysteriously. No one has ever been able to find a trace of it."

"Can't a messenger be sent to the Elf King for help?" insisted Amy.

"Ah, my child, that would have been done long ago had it been possible; but we cannot reach them through the barrier that separates us from their dimension. Only the blasts of the Horn are audible to them. If only we could find it, we could summon King Elfin who would send the wicked gnomes back into their caverns and tunnels forever and prevent any more mischief."

"I can't remember. I can't remember. I just don't know whether he even *said* where he had been," groaned Peter.

"Well," sighed Grandmother, "we must try to save Santa ourselves, then, as best we can. I'll pack a basket of provisions. We must start at once. It will be a long and difficult journey through the snowy woods, for we shall never be able to get there before nightfall. Perhaps if we can warn Santa in time, he may find a way to get you home."

Within an hour preparations for the journey were completed. Peter and Amy carried a picnic basket of food between them. Grandmother brought blankets and a sack containing other useful items. The three emerged from the warm Inn into the bright, cold sunshine. Grandmother closed the door of the Inn behind them, and fitting a huge brass key into the lock, turned it so that no one could enter the Inn from the outside. Then she slipped the key into the pocket of her coat and the three travelers took off across the smooth, deep snow. They followed the footprints of Klutter and Klatter. Homer crouched in the deep windowsill and watched the little party disappear among the trees of the Great Forest.

"Goodness gracious me!" squealed Mistress Mousie.

Chapter 4
King Dock

EANWHILE MISTRESS MOUSIE WAS SCURRYING through the Great Forest as fast as she could run. By the time the winter sun was halfway in its journey across the sky, she had arrived, breathless and excited, at the palace of the Mouse King. She pulled a rope that rang the bell at the gate. A mouse soldier came to the gate to inquire who was there.

"Please tell King Dock that Mistress Mousie has an important message and must see him at once," she squeaked breathlessly, somewhat surprised at her own boldness.

"Do you have an appointment?" asked the soldier.

"Certainly not. This is an urgent matter of national security. A very important person is in grave danger of being kidnapped, along with all his subjects."

The mouse soldier opened the gate.

"Come in," he said. "Wait here."

He disappeared within the castle while Mistress Mousie waited, nervously twitching her whiskers. After what seemed to her to be a very long time, he reappeared.

"Follow me," he said, motioning her to accompany him. Away they went through a maze of corridors and rooms, until they finally arrived at the great hall of the palace. There were mice everywhere clad in rich garments of satins and velvets and delicate silks and laces. At the extreme end of the hall on a splendid golden throne sat King Dock IV.

At any other time Mistress Mousie would have been overwhelmed by the pomp and splendor of the court. But now the urgency of her business gave her courage to overcome her natural timidity. The mouse soldier led her straight to the foot of the royal throne. Mistress Mousie remembered to make a very low curtsey.

"Well, well, Mistress Mousie," said King Dock in a surprisingly deep voice for a mouse. "What errand has brought you so far in such cold winter weather? Whatever it is, it must be very important." The mouse king smiled at her kindly and leaned forward on his throne to hear her reply.

"It is indeed, Your Majesty," squeaked Mistress Mousie. "Last night at the Gingerbread Inn where I live, there were two visitors. Homer, the cat, who is not a bad cat, overheard them plotting to kidnap Santa Claus and enslave all his dwarfs."

"Ah! So that is it!" The King paused to reflect a few moments. Then he addressed her. "As you say, Homer is not a bad cat, as cats go, that is. But cats cannot always be trusted when it comes to mice and birds. Do you think he was inventing this story?"

"The strangers were two gnomes, Klutter and Klatter."

"Klutter and Klatter, the gnomes! That does sound plausible," mused Dock. "In fact, it all makes sense. Perhaps it is true."

"Yes, Your Majesty. Homer also said that Klutter has been guarding the Golden Horn."

"What!" cried the King, half rising from his throne. "The Golden Horn! The gnomes, then, have it! Just as I have always suspected! But then, what if the cat were making up this tale to cause fighting and enmity in the Great Forest?"

"Oh, I do not think so, Your Majesty. Homer is a very good cat. He once rescued one of my babies from Burt the Jay and carried her home in his mouth without harming so much as a hair and left her right at my doorway."

"If all this is as you say, we must make an investigation. What say you, gentlemen? You have all heard. What do you think?" He addressed the mouse lords who had gathered around the throne.

"Did the cat say *how* the gnomes are planning to capture Kris Kringle?" asked Duke Hickory, who wore a patch over one eye and had a gold artificial leg. Everyone looked at Mistress Mousie.

"They are about to purchase a great net — a web that has been spun by the Black Widows. Anything that becomes entangled in this web can never get free. That is what they intend to use on Santa and the dwarfs."

Murmurs of amazement and fear filled the great hall.

24

"This is a gnomes' plot indeed!" cried King Dock. "We must warn Santa at once! Then we must gather together the inhabitants of the Great Forest and plan how we can recover the Golden Horn, which is rightfully ours."

"Have you forgotten, Your Majesty, how difficult it will be for us to communicate with Santa and the dwarfs?" inquired an old mouse lord who had a long white beard and wore velvet knee breeches of an antique style and great horn-rimmed spectacles. "We of the animal kingdom can understand human beings, as well as gnomes, elves, and dwarfs; but we have never found a way of making them really understand our language."

"There will be a problem in communication, Lord Dickory," agreed the King, "which we *must* solve first."

At that moment the Crown Princess stepped up beside her father. She was a beautiful little mouse whose soft gray complexion was elegantly set off by the lovely pastel gowns she invariably wore to court.

"Father, dear," she said sweetly, "why not send a messenger to Santa's reindeer? We *can* tell them about the plot. They will surely find a way to warn Santa before it is too late."

Murmurs of approval rippled through the hall.

"An excellent suggestion, my darling," cried King Dock. "How say you, lords and ladies?"

All agreed that Princess Ittypoo had a capital idea. The King gave orders to a young captain to take a mustoon of mice and go in search of the reindeer immediately.

"And now let us retire to our various apartments to think these problems through, and let us convene in the State Council Chamber at four o'clock to determine upon a plan of action."

Bowing to his courtiers and their ladies, he swept down the aisle they made for him and disappeared through the doorway. Princess Ittypoo turned to Mistress Mousie.

"You have done a wise and brave deed today, Mistress Mousie," she said. "Won't you join us for lunch and then rest yourself awhile before returning to the Gingerbread Inn?"

"No, thank you, Your Royal Highness, I must be getting home. My wee ones will be wondering where I am. They will be cold and hungry and frightened."

"Very well, then, go. But at least let our chef give you a basket of cheese and meal cakes to take with you."

Mistress Mousie thanked the Princess, and taking the basket of provisions, followed the mouse guard back to the palace gate. She scampered through the Forest, never once stopping to rest until she reached the Gingerbread Inn. Squeezing through the crack under the kitchen door, she tiptoed softly to her own little "front door" in the wall beside the fireplace.

Homer was snoozing before the glowing embers on the hearth. She was very careful not to awaken him. After all, he would want to talk, and she knew her hungry children needed her.

Chapter 5
The Black Widows' Web

KLUTTER AND KLATTER, HAVING MADE SO EARLY A START, arrived at the cavern entrance to the Gnome Kingdom by midday. They entered the dark cave, and after walking through underground tunnels for about an hour, during which time they took many twists and turns, for they well knew the route, they arrived at a wall of solid rock. Klutter took a whistle from his pocket and blew a secret tune upon it. The notes were so high pitched that no human ear could hear them. Gnomes, however, have hearing as sharp as a dog's, and to them the sound was quite audible. Some answering notes came through the solid rock. The wall began to swing slowly around, as if it were on pivots. As soon as the opening was several feet wide, Klutter and Klatter squeezed through. The rock wall slammed shut behind them. Klutter and Klatter were in the underground kingdom of the gnomes.

Gnomes were everywhere. It was market day, and some were manning stalls, hawking everything from cabbages and cheese to ruby rings and seven league boots. A crowd had gathered around a little stage where a puppet show was being presented. A parade of gnome soldiers was marching toward the royal palace. They were beating huge metal drums and cymbals and blowing shrill fifes and horns. The noise would have deafened anyone but a gnome.

Klatter and Klutter blended into the crowd of spectators who were all drifting toward the palace. Everyone was discussing the impending appearance of the gnome king and speculating on what the secret weapon would prove to be. Gossip had been flying around, and the gnomes were laying wagers, as they liked nothing better than gambling. An official announcement had been made that very morning that King Klutch would make a public appearance upon the balcony of the palace at noon to speak to his subjects about a matter of great importance and to introduce to them some distinguished visitors to the kingdom.

By the time the gnome subjects had gathered in the vast Palace Square, it was time for the ceremony to begin. The French doors leading to the balcony opened and four gnome pages appeared. After blowing a fanfare on four long golden trumpets, they withdrew and King Klutch himself stepped through the doorway. A great cheer arose from the crowd below, accompanied by a terrible banging and clattering, as the gnomes pounded on drums and brass discs and anything else they had at hand with their spades and axes, for they were never happier than when they were making a horrendous cacophony. When finally they began to quiet down a little, the King raised his right hand and silence fell upon the throng.

"My loyal subjects," began King Klutch, "today we are about to triumph over our age-old enemies — Santa Claus and the dwarfs!"

Wild cheers filled the vast cavern for at least five minutes. Order was finally restored again, and the King continued:

"For centuries our world-design has been thwarted by these stupid creatures whom mortals continue to believe in and to love. No matter how often we have demonstrated the folly and actual harm that this foolish mythology brings, humans continue to ignore the facts and go on living a life of hopes and dreams and love and ridiculous generosity.

"Now at last we have within our power the means to rid the Great Forest of these creatures forever and to save the mortals from the perpetuation of this nonsensical damage."

Again cheers rang through the cavern.

"Now we will introduce to you the one who is to be responsible for our final triumph — the Queen of the Black Widows herself."

What began as a cheer tapered off into a frightened murmur, as the Black Widow Queen sidled through the doorway and joined the King upon the balcony. So fearsome was her face that the gnomes trembled.

"Do you have the secret weapon, gracious Queen?" asked Klutch.

"It is here, Your Majesty." Her voice was taut and silky smooth as she extended toward him a box two feet high, two feet long, and two feet deep.

"Is *that* all there is to it?" asked Klutch.

"It is a very fine web," she replied, "so fine that it is almost invisible, and so it folds up into a very compact bundle. But do not be misled by its present size. It will unfold to a diameter of more than one hundred feet. Only let me warn you and your people. Although it is folded because it does not adhere to itself, it will stick to any living thing that touches its threads, and they will never be able to get free again. It can be neither broken, cut, nor burned. They will be trapped forever.

"When your gnomes are ready to unpack and spread it, they must take care to touch no part of it but the safe green handholds."

A shiver of terror swept through the gnomes, and even King Klutch drew back from the evil Queen.

"And now —" she said, her eyes glittering with the light of greed, as she rubbed her hands together in anticipation, "the payment!"

"Oh, yes," replied King Klutch. He sighed audibly at the thought of parting with so vast a treasure, but he motioned to several gnomes who were holding heavy sacks of gold and gems to approach. "Your price is exorbitant."

"Ha, ha, ha!" laughed the Queen. "It is a *bargain*, considering what *you* will gain. You and your gnomes will rule the world, and you say my price is high! You old — penny pincher!"

Klutch scowled darkly. He was obviously not pleased by the Queen's insulting remarks, however true they were.

"Open the sacks. The payment must be counted," ordered the Queen.

When the sacks were untied and opened, even the Black Widows were speechless at the sight of so much wealth. The gnomes groaned aloud at the thought of parting with so vast a sum that had all been collected from them in taxes. Soon, however, it was all counted and found to be correct. The Black Widows fastened the mouths of the bags, and then began the slow and arduous task of pushing and pulling the treasure toward the entrance of the cavern. Once again the great wall turned on its pivot until the last sack had been dragged outside and the last Black Widow had slipped through the entrance. Then the wall clanged shut, and once again the Gnome Kingdom was sealed off from the Great Forest.

King Klutch again addressed the gnomes:

"My spies have informed me that tomorrow night Santa Claus will hold his annual meeting with the dwarfs in the Council Circle to work out the Christmas Eve Distribution Plan. We shall hide in the treetops about the Circle, and when they have all arrived, we'll lower the net. Tomorrow night we'll capture them all and be masters of the Great Forest forever!"

A loud cheering rang throughout the cavern.

"And now I need one hundred volunteers," said Klutch. "Who will step forward?"

The gnomes drew back. They were, like all such creatures, a cowardly lot. But the King offered generous bribes, so he was eventually able to recruit his "volunteers." After the hundred had been found, Klutter and Klatter offered their services as messengers or trouble shooters. Everything having been arranged, the crowd dispersed. King Klutch, along with his soldiers and volunteers, retired into the castle.

Chapter 6
In the Great Forest

PETER AND AMY AND GRANDMOTHER HOLLYBERRY trudged on through the snow. Since there was only a narrow woodland trail to follow, their progress was extremely slow.

"How long will it take us to get to Santa Claus's house?" asked Peter, who had already forgotten that he had stopped believing in Santa.

"Unless we can find help, it may take us two days," replied Grandmother Hollyberry.

"In that case we may not get there in time."

"I thought Santa lived at the North Pole," remarked Amy.

Grandmother Hollyberry smiled.

"That's just a fairy tale, Amy," she explained. "Somebody who didn't know where Santa *really* lived started that story. Like so many other such tales that are not factual, it just 'caught on' you might say. Soon everybody began telling it, and when enough people go around saying the same thing, they soon convince themselves that it is true, even though there may not be a shred of truth in it.

"When Santa heard that children everywhere were believing his home was at the North Pole, he was at first quite upset, since he didn't want parents to tell untruths to their children because of him. He fretted about the problem until one day one of his dwarfs gave him an idea. It was Clever who suggested to Santa that he change the name of his estate to 'North Pole'. Then it could truthfully be said that he lived there — even though it would not be located at the spot that is officially designated the North Pole of the earth.

"Since there is really no pole running through the earth anyway, and therefore in truth no 'north' or 'south' pole, Santa felt

31

that this would set the matter aright. So he promptly changed the name from Lostlorian to North Pole, and his estate, which is located on a high mountain, has ever since been called that."

"Great jumping beans!" exclained Peter, whistling through his teeth. "We're certainly learning a lot! Wait till the gang hears about *this*!"

"Tell us about North Pole, Grandmother," requested Amy. "Does Santa really make all the toys, or do the dwarfs make them?"

"Santa runs the entire Enterprise. Naturally he does not make each and every toy that mortal children receive on Christmas. Santa is the mastermind behind the entire operation. He is the Spirit of Christmas, and it is he and his dwarfs who send this spirit into your dimension.

"Haven't you noticed how people are transformed at Christmas time? How they become pleasanter and kinder to one another and more thoughtful of the old, the poor, and the sick? Most important of all, they become more charitable. They give unselfishly, often far more than they can well afford to give. It is this Spirit of Love and Generosity that Santa creates and is responsible for. Because mortals give out of love and generosity, they become better than they were before, and thus for a little while, the whole world becomes better, too."

"What do the dwarfs do?" asked Peter softly. "What are they like?"

"You'll see some soon. They have very bright eyes, and they laugh a great deal and sing happy songs. They keep busy planning Christmas, inventing new toys for children and new ways to make them and their parents happy. Their job is also to expedite Christmas Spirit into the world of human beings. Theirs is a great responsibility, for they are charged with the duty of making Christmas merry for every single person who celebrates the Noel. Sometimes they fail, simply because of the occurrence of unhappy events that are outside of their control. But they always do their best — which is very good indeed — and to most mortals they succeed in bringing Christmas Joy."

"It will really be terrible for everybody if the gnomes destroy Santa, won't it?" mused Peter, half to himself.

"They will destroy the Prime Mover — the Spirit of Christmas — all the joy and love of the Holiday Season," said Grandmother.

"Then we'll just have to stop them!" declared Amy.

"We'll do our best, children."

They walked on in silence for quite awhile. The land was becoming hilly and the walking became even more difficult. North Wind was stirring again, and low-hanging clouds were blotting out the sun. Still, on they went, until finally Grandmother Hollyberry called a halt.

"It is nearly four o'clock. In an hour it will be dark. We'll never make North Pole tonight. It looks as though North Wind is planning to bring us snow again. So we had better stop here in this grove of hemlock and build a lean-to for shelter for the night."

She took a hatchet from the basket and began to trim the lower branches from some of the evergreens. Then she showed Peter how to stack them and tie them together to make a secure shelter. Amy gathered firewood, being careful not to wander out of sight. So by the time darkness had completely fallen, the three adventurers had a snug shelter and a bright, warm fire. They were thoroughly exhausted from fatigue, cold, and hunger, since they had had nothing to eat since breakfast.

Grandmother Hollyberry unpacked the food, which she warmed over the fire. She served bowls of steaming Brunswick stew. There was gingerbread, too, and good, hot elflower tea.

Everyone ate heartily, reveling in the warmth of the delicious hot food and the crackling fire. After supper they piled on more wood and crawled into the lean-to. Rolling up in the soft blankets that were made of the wool of the Lost Sheep, they were soon fast asleep. North Wind blew more snow into the Great Forest, but try as he might, he was able to do no harm to our friends. The dense hemlock boughs protected them from both snow and wind, and they slept peacefully until morning.

Once again the sun arose, stretching its fingers of light through the woodland. The snow clouds had passed on and the sky was crystal clear. But the woods were very, very cold.

"We must re-build the fire at once," said Grandmother Hollyberry, "or we may be in danger of freezing."

33

Peter was so cold he could barely feel his fingers and toes, but he set to work gathering more wood and soon Grandmother had a blaze going. They warmed themselves and cooked bacon and oatmeal and made fresh elflower tea.

"We still have about ten miles to walk," said Grandmother, "and the walking will be more difficult as we are getting into mountainous terrain. Let us not linger by the fire. There is no more food or drink. Therefore, we must push on, since we must reach North Pole today before another night comes. We shall leave the baskets; but take your blankets, for they will help to keep you warm and we may need them."

After carefully extinguishing the fire, the three set out once again in the direction that Grandmother Hollyberry pointed out.

❦

Meanwhile Homer drowsed and waited for news from Mistress Mousie. Grandmother Hollyberry had thoughtfully filled his bowl with fresh cream and in another saucer she had left some minced salmon. However, when no one returned by evening, he became very nervous, for he had no way of knowing what was going on. All he could hear was the tick-tock of the grandfather clock in the corner as the new storm swirled around the house. The fire in the hearth was now nothing more than a layer of glowing embers which were slowly blinking out, and the Inn was becoming unbearably cold. As darkness closed in, Homer could stand the strain no longer. He went to the mouse hole and gave a great "merrorrowrr!"

Mistress Mousie popped her head out of the hole immediately.

"Goodness gracious me!" she gasped. "How you did startle me, Homer! I was just coming out to gather some provisions."

"Well, come on, then," replied Homer somewhat gruffly, as he stepped back from the mouse hole. "I've been waiting to hear what happened. Are the mice going to help us?"

"You were asleep when I returned, so I didn't disturb you," said Mistress Mousie, a little defensively.

Mistress Mousie liked Homer and trusted him, but she couldn't resist the temptation to tease him a little. She knew very

34

well how anxious he was, but she took time to set down her basket and smooth out her skirt and re-tie the ribbons on her bonnet before she replied. Homer's eyes glittered impatiently, for he knew she was being deliberately slow in replying. At last she began:

"It took me all morning to reach the Palace. I was simply exhausted when I arrived. At first I thought they weren't going to let me in."

Homer clicked his teeth and flexed his claws to show his impatience.

"Well, when I told them it was a matter of national security, they decided to take me to King Dock himself. Can you imagine *me* Homer, talking to the *King?*"

She paused. "Get on with the story," Homer growled.

"You should have seen all the mouse court. Such clothes! All the latest styles — and jewels! Princess Ittypoo was there. Oh, Homer, you can't believe how beautiful and sweet she is!"

Homer could restrain himself no longer. With lightning swiftness he grabbed Mistress Mousie with both paws, being careful to keep his claws tucked in, and putting his nose against hers said,

"Now *tell* me what they are going to do!"

"All right, all right, Homer. I was just getting to that part."

Then she recounted the entire story, and Homer relaxed his grip.

"So they are going to warn the reindeer," he mused. "Well, that may help. But then again, it may not. The reindeer will have to rescue Santa; but they may not be able to do it. There is the time element. Klutter and Klatter said the kidnapping is to take place tomorrow."

"Well, Homer, that is all I know. King Dock called a Council Meeting at four o'clock, so perhaps they will be able to devise a better plan. Now I must find some cheese and bread for supper."

"It's on the table," said Homer, knowing full well that Grandmother Hollyberry would not forget to leave out some morsels for the little children of Mother Nature during the bitter cold of winter. He went to his own food and ate and drank until he was

35

satisfied. Then he proceeded to wash his face and paws. He took a long drink of the Water of the Crystal Brook that was in his bowl. Jumping onto the back of a chair, he peered out a window into the darkness and swirling snow and decided to wait until sunrise.

As soon as the first light appeared in the sky, Homer went to the door. Standing on his hind legs, he attempted to turn the knob as he had so often seen Grandmother do. He found that his soft little paws just slipped around, and the door knob refused to turn. Then he went to the kitchen door. Mistress Mousie was accustomed to going and coming through the crack under that door, but Homer could do no better than wedge his front paws through. The windows were all closed and latched securely. He tried them all.

At last he came to the upstairs window that the North Wind had broken. He peered out through the hole where the pane was missing, down the steeply slanting roof. It was a long slide and drop to the ground; but North Wind had unintentionally helped him by piling up a huge snowdrift below.

Homer shivered. He thought of food bowls with cream and fish and of how cold and hungry he would be in the Great Forest. But he also thought of Grandmother Hollyberry who was somewhere in those woods on a desperate mission. He thought of the danger to them all. He made his final decision. Squeezing himself through the opening, he slid down the steep, snow-covered roof. There was no turning back now. As he reached the edge he closed his eyes and gave a spring. He landed feet-first in the drift below.

Scrambling out was not easy, but he finally accomplished it. The snow had enough crust upon it for a cat to walk upon. Since he was not sinking in, Homer gathered his feet beneath him and took off pell mell in the direction of North Pole.

Chapter 7
North Pole

PETER AND AMY AND GRANDMOTHER HOLLYBERRY struggled along over the snow. Sometimes it was necessary to clamber over boulders, and once they had to cross a wide river. Fortunately the water was solidly frozen, and they were able to slide all the way across.

About mid-morning they saw ahead of them a mountain range running along the horizon as far as the eye could see. The slopes were densely covered with both deciduous trees and evergreens. One peak rose above all the others and that, Grandmother Hollyberry indicated, was the location of North Pole.

"It is still a long way off, and the hardest part will be climbing the snow-covered mountains," said Grandmother.

They quickened their steps, for they were encouraged by the sight of their destination. After walking another hour, they became aware of the elevation in the land and they realized that they were beginning the final ascent up the mountain. The walking became more and more difficult. They found themselves slipping on icy patches so often that they had to proceed on hands and knees, clutching roots, rocks, and bushes to keep from sliding back down the mountain. At last after great effort they reached a small level area and paused to catch their breath.

Peter walked to the edge and pushing aside some scrubby pines looked out across the valley. He was standing at the rim of a great chasm. A thousand feet below him lay a valley floor strewn with giant boulders. Peter drew back quickly. Amy stared toward him.

"What's down there?" she asked.

"Nothing but rocks. Stay away from the edge," he cautioned.

"That is the Valley of the Trolls," said Grandmother Hollyberry. "Nobody ever goes down there if he can help it."

"What's that noise?" asked Peter.

Everyone listened as the sound grew nearer. Soon it was plain that some sort of four-footed animal was coming down the mountain toward them. In several more minutes a handsome horse with golden saddle and bridle came galloping through the thicket. The most amazing thing about him was his color, for he was a bright red.

"Why, it's Rondo, Santa's own horse!" cried Grandmother.

"Great jumping beans! I never saw a red horse before!" cried Peter.

"I thought Santa had reindeer!" cried Amy.

Rondo neighed in greeting and gave Amy a horsey grin.

"Rondo," said Grandmother Hollyberry, "we have come through the snow all the way from the Gingerbread Inn to warn Santa of a plot the gnomes have devised. We must get to him soon, or it may be too late. Can you help us?"

Now even though animals cannot converse with us, they understand much that we say. Rondo neighed and tossed his head. He took Amy's coat sleeve in his teeth and gently pulled her toward him.

"He wants us to mount," said Grandmother. Peter helped Amy and Grandmother into the saddle, but Rondo refused to move. He tossed his head toward Peter. Climbing upon a rock, Peter hoisted himself over Rondo's broad hind quarters, and the horse took off at a brisk, sure trot. In no time they were on a trail that led steadily upward. At times they came to switchbacks and S curves and the spectacle of the abyss below made them gasp and hang on a little tighter. Yet at no time did Rondo stumble or slip, and after an hour or so they climbed the last few hundred yards and came upon the vast, broad meadow at the top of the mountain. Straight before them rose the walls and gleaming turrets of Santa Claus's white marble castle, which stood in the center of North Pole surrounded by the homes and shops of the dwarfs.

They approached a heavy wrought-iron gate. A guard allowed them to enter, and suddenly they were cantering noisily up the cobble-stoned Main Street of North Pole. The dwarfs lived in quaint mushroom-shaped dwellings. Little dwarfs were romping in the snow or skating on a nearby pond. Their mothers and fathers were busily going about their usual tasks in the numerous mushroom-shaped workshops that nestled here and there among the homes.

Everyone stopped and stared at the riders on Rondo's back, but the red horse never slackened his gait until he paused at last before the castle door.

"I can't believe this is all really real," said Peter, mostly to himself.

Rondo pulled a bell rope with his teeth and the door swung open. A dwarf guard allowed them to enter.

"We wish to see Santa Claus at once," said Grandmother Hollyberry.

"Santa Claus is meeting with the Steering Committee and cannot be disturbed. They are planning the Annual Christmas Council Meeting that is to be held at Hemlock Circle at eight o'clock tonight."

"We *must* see him," insisted Peter. "The gnomes are plotting to capture all of you with a secret weapon and destroy Christmas forever."

"What? Is this true?"

Grandmother Hollyberry nodded. "It is just as Peter says. We have come on foot all the way from the Gingerbread Inn to warn you."

"How did these mortal children get here?" asked the dwarf.

"They 'slipped through' somehow."

"We really want to get home," apologized Amy.

"Wait here," said the dwarf.

Peter, Amy, and Grandmother Hollyberry dismounted from Rondo's back.

"Good boy!" said Peter, patting the horse's nose. Rondo nuzzled Peter and nickered softly. In a few minutes the dwarf returned.

"Come right this way," he motioned and padded off down the thickly carpeted hall. They came at last to a huge sliding door. The dwarf grasped a heavy brass ring and with some effort slid the door back. Before them in a richly paneled room, seated at the head of a huge oak table, sat Santa Claus himself. Ten dwarf councilors were seated around the table, which was covered with papers and maps.

"Master Peter, Mistress Amy, and Grandmother Hollyberry," announced the first dwarf, "to see Santa Claus."

"Well, come in, come in!" called Santa in a gruff but kindly tone. "So you have come through blizzards from the Gingerbread Inn to warn me of a plot, have you? Don't stand *there*. Come right over here and sit down beside me. There now. Bring them some warm food and drink and let us all hear what you have to say."

Then Grandmother Hollyberry explained how Peter and Amy had arrived at the Inn, how she had fed them and put them to bed, the arrival of the hooded travelers during the storm, and how Peter, getting up for a drink of water during the night, had overheard the plot.

Santa asked Peter to recount every single word he had heard. Peter tried hard to remember everything, but he could not recall where Klutter said he had been guarding the Golden Horn.

"Did they *really* speak of the Golden Horn?" asked Santa, leaning down close to Peter.

"Yes, sir," replied Peter.

"Ho! ho! ho!" chuckled Santa, "So the gnomes are the scamps who have it! Just as soon as Christmas is over, we must figure out a way to get it back. Now, Sonny, if *only* you could recall *where* he said he was guarding it, we would be a little closer to safety."

"I can't remember. I'm not even sure that he *said* where he had been." Peter frowned deeply, as if frowning might help him to recollect.

"Well, we must let it go for the moment. At eight tonight, we shall all assemble at Hemlock Circle. All the plans are ready. Assignments and maps are prepared for distribution. Each dwarf will be given his own individual assignment for this Holiday Season."

"But Santa," objected an old dwarf, "What about this plot to destroy us? Hadn't we better take some precautions? This 'secret weapon' — what might it be? How might it be used?"

Santa shrugged. "What would you suggest? We have no idea what they are up to. We can't just sit and wait — there is too much to do. How can we take action when nothing has occurred?"

"It might be a good idea to hold the Council Meeting within the walls and post guards to keep a sharp eye on things," suggested the young dwarf named Clever.

"There is no space in the town large enough for a convention," objected Santa. "We can't postpone the meeting because there is not enough time. However, we can bring arms, and we can post a guard. That is about the best we can do. The gnomes are very cunning. There is no predicting what sort of mischief they may have in store for us."

Then he turned to the children.

"You two stay in the Castle tonight with Grandmother Hollyberry. No matter what — if anything — may happen, you'll be safe here."

"Santa," asked Peter. "do you think you can help us get home after the meeting? Everybody in the Great Forest has been good to us, but, you see, we sort of miss Mom and Dad."

Santa spread his fingers on the table and regarded them thoughtfully. "It won't be easy," he mused. "But I know your parents are deeply concerned about you, and there is a search going on right now, and you want to be with them. If you can ride through the air on the reindeer, perhaps we can get you there Christmas Eve."

"Oh, yes, we can! We can!" cried Amy, jumping up and down and clapping her hands.

"Then we shall try," agreed Santa. "Now let us have some supper. All our preparations are complete."

Homer crept warily along the edge of the main road.

Chapter 8
In the South Tunnel

T HE NIGHT WAS DARK. Heavy clouds had gathered over the mountain top. Not a single star was shining.

Peter and Amy stood together at the tower window and watched the dwarfs as they came from every direction to join the long line that was slowly moving through the gates of the outer wall and across the broad meadows toward Hemlock Circle. There were hundreds of dwarfs — young and old, tall and short, stout and thin, hairy and bald. Each was colorfully attired in full knee breeches, high black leather boots, warm jerkins, and the typical pointed cap that male dwarfs always wear. Tonight they wore thick woolen mittens to protect their hands from the cold. Each dwarf carried some sort of weapon — an ax, a shovel, a hammer, or even a knife. In his other hand he carried by a large brass ring a lanthorn in which a tallow candle was burning brightly.

The mothers and little ones stood at their cottage doors and waved good-bye. Usually this evening of the annual Council Meeting at Hemlock Circle was a jolly occasion. The dwarfs would have been singing or telling jokes to each other. Tonight, however, they walked silently in fear. Word of the gnomes' treachery had spread. No one knew what the secret weapon would prove to be, and this lack of knowledge made the possibility more frightening rather than less so. Hence, the dwarfs talked softly and walked armed. As they passed through the gates and into the meadow, they conversed only in subdued whispers, because they were listening for the slightest sound that might reveal the presence of the gnomes.

Peter and Amy watched them go. Out through the gate and across the darkness of the snow-covered meadows they filed, the lights from their lanthorns streaming out like a trail of little stars. The trail led nearly a mile to the great circle of giant hemlocks which was known as Hemlock Council Circle. Soon the lights bobbed and flickered about the bases of the trees as the dwarfs assembled and took their places. Then the children saw Santa Claus followed by his ten councilors. Santa was riding Rondo, who was stepping along at a rather brisk gait.

At last all were gathered within the circle of trees. The bobbing lights became still as the dwarfs seated themselves on the ground. Santa, who was seated with the councilors on a platform that had been erected for the occasion, rose to speak. He had no sooner begun when suddenly the sound of thundering hooves caused everyone to freeze and look in the direction of the noise. In another moment a herd of reindeer burst from the forest and galloped straight across the meadow toward the circle of lights. When they reached the giant hemlocks, they paused in their wild flight. Then each deer stepped into the Circle, and one trotted briskly up to Santa.

"Whatever is the meaing of this, Donder?" cried Santa. "Why have you all rushed in here to interrupt our meeting?"

Alas, Donder couldn't talk. He pushed Santa with his nose. He pawed the air. He tossed his head. Then the other reindeer formed a circle and lowering their heads, allowed their antlers to touch. The antlers formed a kind of interlinking net.

The dwarfs were chattering excitedly now. Everyone realized that the deer were trying to convey a message. Everyone was trying to guess what it was. Suddenly Clever cried,

"I have it! The gnomes have a net!"

All the reindeer nodded.

"But a net — what harm could a net do?" asked Santa.

The reindeer became frantic. They began to gently push the dwarfs with their antlers toward the edge of the Circle in the direction of the town gates.

"Then there *is* danger here!" cried Santa. "Let us be off. But go in an orderly fashion, or you may hurt one another."

At once the dwarfs jumped to their feet, but suddenly a great, filmy, nearly invisible net swiftly descended from above. It floated silently downward from the tops of the eighty-foot trees.

44

Sunshine looked up and saw it.

"Look!" he cried, dropping his lanthorn and pointing above.

Too late. The net had reached its target. Before one single dwarf could escape through the encircling trees, Santa, dwarfs, and reindeer — all — were caught in its sticky folds.

A loud cheer went up from the hemlock trees. As the dwarfs watched helpless from below, there appeared from the dense foliage of every tree gnomes. They were cheering, waving, laughing in triumph as below them, caught forever in the sticky, unbreakable folds of the Black Widows' Web were Santa, the deer, and all the helpless little dwarfs.

"Ho! Ho! Ho!" King Klutch mimicked Santa as he stood on a sturdy branch high above the net. "What do you say now, Kris Kringle? Now we have you all in our power forever!"

"However did you manage this, Klutch?" cried Santa.

"While you and your dwarfs were busy all day working on your various Christmas projects, we crept up the mountain. You had no guard posted, for you never suspected mischief. A corps of volunteers climbed the hemlock trees, each holding a handle of the Black Widows' Web until it was sixty feet or more above the ground and spread over the entire area. North Wind helped us by covering the moon and stars with clouds. The dark net was invisible against the dark sky. So we sat hidden in the high branches and waited for you. *Now* let's hear you say, 'Ho! Ho! Ho!' " mimicked Klutch.

Meanwhile the dwarfs were frantically trying to break free of the net. But even those who had knives were unable to cut a thread of it; and the more they struggled, the more they became stuck to the sticky substance that coated its surface. Seeing their plight, the gnomes set up a howl of laughter and shouting that echoed and re-echoed through the mountains. The more they laughed and howled, the more the dwarfs struggled; while the more they struggled, the more securely trapped they became.

Finally Santa was able to make his own voice heard. He begged the dwarfs and deer to be still, lest they injure one another in their struggles. Then he addressed King Klutch:

"Well, now that we are your prisoners, what is it that you want? If you want toys and gifts on Christmas, we shall bring you some."

Another roar of derisive laughter filled the night. When the gnomes quieted down again, Klutch spoke:

"Santa, you are not merely our prisoners. You are our slaves — forever. We do not want Christmas gifts. Never again will you make people happy with Christmas gifts. You will all be taken to our subterranean caverns where the air is hot and sulphurous. You will be forced to work for *us*, refining our ores in the stifling furnaces, digging deep into hazardous mine shafts, and doing any other dangerous or tedious work that we wish done. We'll find a way to free you of the net and put you all in chains. Never again will you visit humanity on Christmas Eve. Never again will you return to North Pole or see the Great Forest. You will become a myth, and the children will not believe in you any more."

Some of the dwarfs began to cry, and Santa's face showed great concern.

"Surely Klutch, you are not serious?" cried Santa.

"Never more serious in my life, you mischievous red elf," replied Klutch. He waved his arm in the direction of the castle. "The First Brigade is now to proceed according to the plan. Round up the women and children dwarfs and march them down to the Valley of the Trolls. See that no one escapes. The rest of you are to drag the net of prisoners to the entrance to Sulphur Cave and into the subterranean caverns. Come! Let it be done!"

In the town of North Pole the shouts and raucous laughter had been heard. The dwarfs bolted their doors and huddled in fear inside their little mushroom-shaped cottages. The gnomes, however, had little difficulty battering down those doors, and soon enough, the terrified little people were being marched down the snow-covered mountain in the middle of the frigid, dark December night.

Amy and Peter and Grandmother Hollyberry heard all the commotion, too. They realized that the gnomes must have attacked, but they had no way of knowing what was actually going on. As they tried to peer through the frost-coated windowpanes, there came a terrible pounding on the castle door. Soon they heard the sound of running feet in the corridor. Their door burst open and several gnomes rushed in. Too late they tried to escape. They were overtaken quickly and dragged along with the others.

As they were being led from the castle, they encountered Klutter and Klatter, who were in charge of the castle arrests. The two gnomes laughed gleefully when they saw the three prisoners and nudged each other.

"Well, well," said Klutter, "what a prize we have here! Two mortal children and Grandmother Hollyberry herself!"

"You rascals!" cried Grandmother Hollyberry. Leaning forward, she caught Klutter's huge nose and gave it a tweak. "Release us at once! These children are not to be harmed!"

"Take them to King Klutch," ordered Klatter. "What a prize *they'll* be! Old Klutch will probably give us a special reward for real mortal children and Grandmother Hollyberry, no less!" He bowed mockingly.

"I hab a betta idea," said Klutter, who was holding his nose and dancing about because of the pain. "We'll take dem to South Tunnel and keep dem ourselbes for awhile. Perhabs we can find a way to make dem really valuable to us."

"Klutter, you *are* a genius!" exclaimed Klatter with genuine admiration.

Even though the three captives pulled and struggled, they were soon bound like the dwarfs and half dragged, half marched from the castle, across the snowy meadow, along a path that led straight down the forested mountain. The entrance to South Tunnel was in a different direction from Sulphur Cavern, so the three friends with their captors soon separated from the others, taking a little trail that branched off from the main path.

"You'll be sorry about all this when my father hears what you've done," taunted Peter.

"Oh, is that so?" sneered Klutter. "And just how is he to hear? Are you planning to telephone him — long distance, perhaps?"

Klatter snickered.

"Just you wait until Christmas when all the children all over the world wake up and find that Santa hasn't come."

"Yes," agreed Amy, "they'll call out the police and the firemen, and — and — everybody."

"Who's Everybody?" inquired Klatter.

"The Army and the Navy," cried Peter, "and the Air Force and the Marines, too."

"Who's going to do that?" insisted Klutter.

"The President — that's who!" retorted Peter.

"How's he to know where we are?" asked Klatter slyly.

"The F.B.I.'ll tell 'em. *They* can find anybody who's kidnapped or missing."

"What's that?" asked Klutter suspiciously.

"It's their underground organization," replied Klatter.

"Like us?"

"Not exactly. But don't worry. They'll never be able to 'get through'. We're perfectly safe."

"Oh, no, you're not," cried Grandmother Hollyberry. "Evil can never triumph for long in the Great Forest. You may think you're winning now, but it won't be for long."

"Oh, is that so-oo! You old witch! And who do you think will rescue *you*?" said Klatter.

"I don't know 'who' or 'how'," admitted Grandmother, "but I do know that good will triumph, and you and your fellow gnomes will be very, very sorry for your naughtiness."

"Don't you call Grandmother Hollyberry a witch," cried Amy.

But Klatter just gave them a shove and told them to keep quiet and walk faster.

Just as the shining face of the morning sun was peeping through the trunks of the trees, they arrived at the entrance to the South Tunnel. The entrance was low and overhung with stringy vines. Icicles hung from the rocks above the hole. Everyone, even the gnomes, had to crawl on hands and knees through the opening to get inside the cave. It was a rather small cave, no more than twelve or fifteen feet in diameter, with a roof no higher than six feet. A tunnel led off into total darkness straight ahead of them.

"Let's tie them up more securely and leave them here until we can figure out a way to use them," suggested Klutter.

"I'm hungry," complained Amy. "It's time for breakfast."

Klatter sneered. "You'll have to *earn* your breakfast from now on, Miss. You'll work for every crumb you get."

Peter struggled, but the ropes just cut more deeply into his wrists. Seeing how helpless their three prisoners were, Klutter and Klatter laughed in glee and hugged each other.

"Let's leave them awhile and join the others," urged Klutter. "The King has invited us all to the victory celebration and the royal banquet to be held tonight. Every delicacy in the kingdom is being prepared by the royal chefs."

Klatter licked his lips at the thought of so grand a feast.

"Good idea," he said. "But let's put a rock against the entrance, just in case they *should* manage to get those ropes loose. We'll be back for you — later!" He shook his finger at the captives.

The gnomes crawled back through the entrance and, pushing with all their strength, rolled a large boulder against the hole. Our friends were left in nearly total darkness. The only light came through an opening no larger than a saucer where the rock did not quite cover the hole at the top. A beam of sunlight shone through this small space. It shimmered through the icicles that hung down from the rocks above and fell in a golden circle on the floor of the cave. Amy began to cry.

"Do not cry, my dear," said Grandmother Hollyberry. "We must not give up hope. As long as there is a little light, we must not give up hope."

Chapter 9
Homer to the Rescue

MEANWHILE HOMER WAS TROTTING SWIFTLY through the forest. It was bitter cold, but Mother Nature had given him a heavy fur coat which kept him from freezing. The snowfall of the night before had obliterated the footprints of Amy, Peter, and Grandmother Hollyberry; but cats have a remarkable sense of smell, just as dogs have. Even though a mortal would have found it quite impossible to follow a snow-covered trail, Homer had little difficulty picking up the scent through the newly fallen snow.

As the sun rose higher and higher, Homer's spirits rose also. Since he had four legs instead of two, he traveled much more swiftly than our friends. By mid-afternoon he reached the river, where he paused to rest. He was hungry and thirsty, but there was nothing to eat or drink. Suddenly, he heard a rustle in the trees above him. Looking up quickly, he saw a red bird. He thought he recognized it as the bird that Grandmother Hollyberry was accustomed to feeding.

For a few seconds the bird and the cat looked at each other. Homer's natural instincts overwhelmed his better nature, and he clicked his teeth and switched his long, black tail.

"I wouldn't do that if I were you!" chirped the bird.

Homer froze.

"*I'm* Grandmother Hollyberry's pet, too, you know."

Homer sighed and relaxed.

"What are you doing *here*?" he asked.

"I might ask *you* the same question," replied the bird, cocking his head in a saucy manner.

"Grandmother and those two children are trying to save Santa and the dwarfs. The gnomes are planning to kidnap them. I am afraid Grandmother is in great danger."

50

"You are right," replied the bird. "If you will behave yourself and promise never to try to eat me — or my children — *ever* — perhaps I can help all of you."

Homer sighed deeply. It was against his nature to make such a promise. Yet he thought of Grandmother's kindness, as well as of his full bowl and warm bed by the hearth. If he could save all this and all the creatures of the Great Forest, such a promise would, after all, be a small concession to make.

"I promise," he said at last.

"Cross your heart and raise your right paw," insisted the bird.

"Oh, all right. I cross my heart and raise my right paw," said Homer crossly; and he did.

The bird hopped down to a lower limb.

"As I was flying ahead of you up the mountain I met a mustoon of mice. The captain told me that they were in search of Santa's reindeer. They intended to warn the deer of the gnomes' treachery. Santa and his dwarfs plan to hold their annual meeting at Hemlock Circle tonight. The gnomes are already hidden in the thick foliage of the giant hemlock trees. I flew up to the Circle and saw them myself. They arrived before daybreak. They will probably just stay there unnoticed until nightfall. When it is dark again they will spread the circular net. One hundred gnomes will each hold a green handle. They and the net will be high above the ground. When Santa and all the dwarfs are seated within the circle, they will simply let go and the net will float down — trapping Santa and all his dwarfs."

A great shiver of fright went through Homer, rippling his beautiful fur coat.

"What can we do?" asked the cat, half to himself and half to the bird.

The red bird cocked his head and looked down at Homer with one bright little eye.

"There is one thing that might save us all," he said.

"What is that?" asked Homer quickly.

"The Golden Horn."

"The Golden Horn! But Klutter and Klatter say the gnomes have it."

51

"The mice, who have spies everywhere, have discovered where it is hidden."

"They told you?" asked Homer, bending forward tensely.

"It is buried for safe keeping in a cave that is the entrance to the South Tunnel."

"Merowr-r-r!" bawled Homer. Forgetting himself in his excitement, he leaped at the red bird and almost caught him in his forepaws.

The bird flew up to a higher limb just in time.

"What about your promise, you crooked cat?" he squawked angrily. "I never should have trusted *you*!"

"I'm sorry. I really am. I didn't mean to frighten you," apologized Homer. "I really wanted to hug you. Honestly!"

The bird looked at him suspiciously.

"Well, if you're *sure* you didn't mean to have me for lunch —"

"I really had no such thought in mind. Please believe me." Homer was so contrite, that the bird finally forgot his fear and hopped down close to the cat's nose.

"Somehow you must recover the Golden Horn. Even though you may find it, you won't be able to use it. So you must get it to Grandmother, or one of those children, or even a dwarf. But someone must get that Horn who can blow it to summon the elves."

"Yes. You are right. It is the only hope. I must try. It is the least I can do," Homer meowed.

"Do your best, Homer. I shall fly up the mountain again and keep watch on things. If I see the mice again, I'll tell them you're here. And Homer! Do be careful! The fate of the entire Great Forest and the Spirit of Love in the world is in *your* paws."

Then the red bird soared away across the river toward the mountain range that lay ahead. Homer had forgotten his hunger and thirst. Re-doubling his effort, he took off at a swift lope across the ice. Driven by purpose, he ran as he had never run before. Turning neither to right nor left — except to avoid a tree, bush, or boulder — he raced along. He fortunately found the trail up the mountain before he had climbed more than a hundred feet. Running on a trail is easier than charging headlong up a heavily wooded hillside; but as the ascent grew steeper, Homer began to pant for breath. At last he was forced to slow down.

As he followed the hairpin curves and switchbacks of the trail, he gazed dizzily down into the abysses below, and his fur rippled in fright. Unlike most cats, Homer actually feared great heights. He hated to admit this, even to himself, for he considered it very cowardly in a cat. A proper cat, he believed, should feel secure on a limb sixty feet above the ground. Such height he always cautiously avoided, since it made him feel dizzy and nauseated and caused his hide to ripple uncomfortably.

In spite of all his efforts, the sun had set and darkness was falling before he arrived at North Pole. Frozen, starved, and exhausted, he crawled through the bars of the iron gates as the chimes were striking five o'clock. He crept warily along the edge of the main road. He knew he must find Grandmother Hollyberry, but he had no idea where she was.

The little windows of the mushroom houses were brightly lit. Smoke was pouring from the chimneys and carrying with it the delicious aroma of the dwarfs' dinners. A couple of little dwarfs were walking home together. They had been ice skating on the pond in the meadows and had tarried a little too long before starting home. Now with their skates over their shoulders, they were hastening home so as not to be late for dinner.

"Look!" exclaimed one, "There's a cat."

In a moment Homer found himself surrounded.

"He looks like a stray," said the other.

The first dwarf bent over and picked him up.

"Look! His feet are bleeding. There's blood in the snow."

"He looks cold and hungry. Let's take him home. Mommy will give him something to eat."

Now Homer didn't want to be "taken home". He was on a rescue mission. If only he could have told the dwarfs the whole story! But that was impossible. He wriggled and squirmed and tried to get loose, but the little dwarf only held him more tightly. Homer knew he could bite and scratch and get free; but he also knew that this was not proper behavior for a good cat.

"He's really frightened," said the smaller of the dwarfs. "He's afraid of you, Blossom. He's trying to get loose."

53

"I can feel his little heart just pounding," said Blossom. "Let's hurry home with him. I'm not sure how much longer I can hold him."

They trotted along swiftly down the main street past the cobbler's and the green grocer's, and turned off on a side road where they eventually stopped before a neat little mushroom cottage. They entered a warm room. Homer felt grateful for the warmth and began to relax in spite of himself.

"Look, Mommy, we found a lost cat," said the little dwarf called Blossom.

"May we feed him and keep him, Mommy?" asked his little brother.

"A lost cat? He doesn't look like a stray," said the mother dwarf, as she examined Homer. "He's been walking through rough ground and ice and snow, though." She was inspecting his paws. "We'll give him something to eat and drink and let him sleep here tonight; but tomorrow we'll have to try to find his owners."

"Why can't we keep him, Mommy?" asked Bud. "He's ours. We found him!"

"You may not keep him if he belongs to someone else, dear. Right now his owners may be grieving for him or even searching the Great Forest for him. But come now. Here is a bowl. Give him something to eat. You may use the old blanket in the chest to make him a bed by the fire. Then come to the table quickly, or your own supper will be cold."

The little dwarfs scurried about doing as they were bidden, and Homer began to relax in spite of himself. By the time he had eaten and warmed himself, an overpowering weariness began to steal over him.

"After all," he thought, "I don't even know where Grandmother Hollyberry is. I'll have to try to get out of here and find her after they all go to bed. So right now I'll just lie by the fire for a little while and take a short cat nap. I won't close my eyes tightly. I'll watch...and see...see when..." Homer was sound asleep in spite of himself.

Sometime later he was awakened by a pounding on the front door. He heard a great din outside. He opened his eyes and for a moment wondered where he was. Then he saw the two dwarf children and their mother standing by the door as the gnomes forced it open and pushed their way into the house. Instinctively Homer leaped for the mantel above the hearth. A large clock stood at one end. Homer crawled behind it and tucked in his tail. No one noticed him in the excitement. He watched in terror as the dwarfs were marched away.

Frightened as he was, he knew he couldn't stay there. Somehow he *must* find Grandmother Hollyberry. He hid for a few minutes longer, and then jumping down, he slipped cautiously through the half-open door into the darkness outside. Gnomes were everywhere, leading their captives away through the town gates across the Meadows to the trail which led down the mountain. Homer climbed a cedar tree. Safely hidden by the heavy green foliage, he could watch the procession without being seen.

Suddenly his little heart stopped beating. There were Klutter and Klatter leading Grandmother, Amy, and Peter. They passed right beside him as he crouched on a limb scarcely daring to breathe. He knew that he must follow them without being detected by the gnomes. At least they hadn't been caught in the net! Had they been trapped in the sticky folds of the Black Widows' web, the problem of rescue might have been utterly hopeless.

Homer scrambled to the ground, and keeping a safe distance from the crowd, inched his way along, taking care never to lose sight of the five figures ahead. His black and white coat did give him the advantages of a natural camouflage against the white snow in a pitch black winter night.

Thus he crept along, always keeping far enough away to avoid detection. When the gnomes and their three captives separated from the others, Homer turned to follow. Once he slipped on the side of an icy boulder and slid and rolled several hundred feet down the mountain before a thick bush fortunately checked his fall. He looked over his shoulder. Below him was the Valley of the Trolls. He was right on the edge of the abyss. Homer yowled in terror. He forgot the need to be quiet. He was afraid to move for fear he would slip on the crusty snow and slide right over the edge. He clutched at the bush with all his claws and closed his eyes and wailed. Fortunately, no one heard him.

Gradually his terror subsided a bit, and again he opened his eyes. He ventured to look over the edge, and again the fear swept over him. He knew, however, that he couldn't stay there forever. He looked back up the steep slope he had slid down. Above and to the left there was a large, flat boulder. If he could just climb to that rock, he would be a little safer. The thought of letting go of the bush was terrifying. But he had to do something. He would try to make it.

Very carefully he pushed one forepaw deeply into the crusty snow. Then he pushed the other ahead of it. He dug in his hind feet as hard as he could. Again he inched up and over. By now he was free of the bush. There was nothing to stop him if he slipped. For a second he almost panicked. Scarcely daring to breathe, he kept going — up and over. In thirty seconds he had made it to the rock. An old fallen pine tree lay against the boulder. Its long trunk made a safe road back up the slope, for the little cat could use his claws on the wood to keep from slipping. It was not more than a few minutes before Homer had picked up the trail again.

So he followed Klutter, Klatter, Grandmother Hollyberry, Peter and Amy straight down the mountain to the entrance of the caves. When the gnomes pushed their three captives into the cave, Homer crawled to the rock above and tried to listen to what was transpiring inside. All he could hear was the murmur of muffled voices. He could not hear what was being said. He was wondering what to do next when suddenly Klutter and Klatter emerged. Homer quickly crouched behind a bush to avoid detection. He saw them roll the boulder into the mouth of the cave and watched as the gnomes tramped off through the Great Forest. At last they were out of sight.

Homer waited only until they were no longer visible. Then he scrambled down from his hideout. He climbed the boulder to the top and peered through the glistening icicles that were suspended from the rock above the entrance. The hole was small and dark. Homer's eyes were not adjusted to the darkness of the cave after the bright morning sunshine and the glistening snow. But he knew his friends were there because his nose told him so.

56

Chapter 10

Discovery

WHEN HOMER PEERED INTO THE CAVE, he cut off a portion of the little pool of sunlight that lay on the ground. Amy was the first to notice and looked up quickly. She was naturally surprised to see the silhouette of a cat's head in the opening above.

"Look!" she exclaimed.

Peter and Grandmother Hollyberry glanced toward the hole.

"It's a cat!" said Peter.

"I do believe — why it is! It's a cat! Why it's Homer!" cried Grandmother Hollyberry.

With that, Homer gave a spring. Icicles splintered and flew in all directions as he hurtled through the opening and landed in Grandmother Hollyberry's lap. The next moment he was rubbing against her and purring as noisily as ever a cat can purr.

"Good Homer! Good Homer!" said Grandmother. "But why did you come here to the South Tunnel? You should have stayed at the Inn where you were safe," she chided.

Homer, however, heard nothing after "South Tunnel." He was electrified by the words. So *that's* where they were! At once he began to scratch and dig up the ground.

"Whatever is wrong with him?" asked Amy, as Homer continued to tear up the hard-packed cave floor with all his might.

"I don't know. I've never seen him behave like that before," mused Grandmother.

"Well, no matter. We'll have to try to get loose," said the practical Peter. "We don't know how long it will be before Klutter and Klatter return. I just remembered — I had my penknife when I left home. If it is still in my pocket, Amy, maybe you can get it out for me. If I can just hump over to where you are — there! Now if you can manage to get your hands in my pocket — "

57

"My hands are in your pocket, but I can't find a knife. Here's a marble."

"There, try it now." Peter moved over.

"I think — I have it!"

"Don't let go!"

"Okay. Now what?" The children were back to back.

"Just slip it into my fingers. Careful now."

"Do you have it?"

"Yes."

"Now what?"

"I've got the blade out. Put your hands over mine so I can saw through the rope. Be careful now. Yell if I start to cut you. Is that you or the rope?"

"I think it must be the rope, but I'm so cold I may not feel it."

Peter cautiously worked the edge of the knife back and forth.

"Don't move now," he cautioned. "I think I'm getting it. Now see if you can break it."

Amy pushed against the rope and it gave enough for her to slip her hands free.

"Hurrah!" cried Peter. "Now take the knife and cut my hands loose. Careful now — ouch! You nicked me!"

"I'm sorry, Peter. Hold still."

At last the ropes were all severed and the captives were at least free of their bonds. They all stood up and stretched and hugged each other in joy.

"Now we must try to push the boulder away and get out of here," said Grandmother Hollyberry.

All the while Homer was digging frantically.

"What's the matter with him?" asked Amy again.

Peter shrugged. "Never mind *him!* Let's all push the rock."

So all three put their hands on the boulder and shoved with all their might, but it refused to budge an inch.

"Oh, dear! I was afraid of this," cried Grandmother Hollyberry. "All of us together are not as strong as one gnome. Klutter and Klatter could easily roll this stone into the entrance, but we'll never be able to shove it out."

"Let's try again," said the dauntless Peter, and once again they shoved with all their strength, but with no more success.

"Where does the South Tunnel lead?" asked Peter.

Grandmother Hollyberry shrugged her shoulders wearily. "Who knows? Perhaps to a dead end, or very possibly directly to an entrance to the Gnome Kingdom."

"What *is* Homer up to?" asked Amy.

The little cat was digging right in the circle of sunlight that fell through the opening onto the ground. As they watched, they suddenly saw something glint in the light. Now Homer's claws were scratching against something hard.

"Maybe it's some of the gnomes' treasure," suggested Amy.

Peter knelt down to investigate. Suddenly he seized a flat stone and began digging also.

"Whatever *is* it, Peter?" asked Grandmother Hollyberry.

"Don't know. But it's big and hard."

Amy picked up another stone and helped dig. Suddenly Peter cried out.

"We've found it! We've found it! It's the Golden Horn! Now I remember hearing Klatter say something about the South Tunnel that night at the Inn. He had been guarding the Horn in the South Tunnel, I suppose."

"Great stars and elflowers!" cried Grandmother Hollyberry. "We're saved! Hurry, Peter, hurry! Finish digging it out. Get it out quickly!"

All four of them now dug frantically with whatever stones they could find, and Homer with his claws. Gradually the beautiful horn was unearthed.

Suddenly Grandmother Hollyberry paused.

"Hark! Someone's coming!"

"It's the gnomes!" she gasped. "They're coming back! Quickly, dear Peter, faster, faster. Now pull — hard!"

They caught hold of the end and pulled, and the horn came free of the earth. Peter held it up and shook out the loose soil. He wanted to wipe it clean, but the others were urging him on.

"Now Peter, you must blow three blasts upon the horn — quickly, quickly!" urged Grandmother Hollyberry.

The voices were louder. They were right outside the cave. Suddenly the boulder began to move as the gnomes pushed upon it. Peter took a deep breath and put the horn to his lips. The boulder rolled back, and the light of day rushed into the cave. There stood Klutter and Klatter.

Peter tipped his head back and blew three strong blasts upon the Golden Horn.

Chapter 11
Stars and Elflowers

KLUTTER AND KLATTER WERE SO STARTLED by the unexpected blast of the Golden Horn that they stopped still right inside the entrance of the cave. Before they could recover from their surprise, a ball of light the size of an orange appeared. It grew larger and larger, like a balloon being inflated. Everyone watched in amazement as the bubble burst into a shower of golden droplets. There before them stood a strikingly handsome young man clad in green from head to foot.

"King Elfin!" cried Grandmother Hollyberry, and she made a deep, old-fashioned curtsey.

"Grandmother Hollyberry!" the King bowed low. "Why have you summoned the elves?"

"Wow!" gasped Peter.

"A real fairy prince!" cried Amy, clapping her hands. But Klutter and Klatter were frozen in terror.

"Your Royal Highness," said Grandmother, "we have summoned you to the Great Forest because we are in mortal danger. The gnomes have acquired a net made by the Black Widows. With this net they have entrapped Santa Claus, along with all his dwarfs and reindeer. Their objectives are to destroy the Spirit of Christmas in the world and to enslave the dwarfs.

"It is they who stole the Golden Horn from Lothra's branch and hid it here so we could not call you and your people to save us."

"Is this indeed true?" cried King Elfin. "Then we must rescue our friends and punish the gnomes for their monstrous deeds. May I have the Horn?"

Peter handed King Elfin the Golden Horn. The King placed the Horn to his lips and blew a fanfare. The tones rang through the cave and outside in the Great Forest. The sound was so clear and musical that the notes rippled through the cold winter air as sunshine sparkles on the waters of the ocean.

61

"Now let us leave this cold, dark cave," said Elfin, and he helped Grandmother Hollyberry and Amy and Peter through the opening.

Klutter and Klatter, seeing a chance to escape, took off down the tunnel as fast as they could run.

"Let them go," said Elfin. "We'll deal with them later."

No sooner had they emerged from the cave than elves began to appear from every direction. A little golden bubble would float into sight, grow larger, explode, and there would be an elf. They stood on the rocks; they sat on the limbs of the spruces and hemlocks; they stood on the snowy ground. They were everywhere — an army of green-clad figures with wings that resembled pieces of the rainbow.

Homer was so unnerved by the throng of strangers that he crawled close to Grandmother Hollyberry. He hoped that these creatures liked cats; but in case they didn't, he would be close to his benefactress.

King Elfin led Grandmother, Peter, and Amy up to a high, flat rock, and addressed the crowd of elves.

"We have been summoned here to the Great Forest, dear friends, because the good little folk who live in this dimension have been captured by the Gnome King. He has used a weapon made by the Black Widows — a web so strong and sticky that anyone caught in it can never escape. This brave boy," he indicated Peter, "was somehow able to recover the Golden Horn, which the gnomes had previously stolen and hidden in the South Tunnel; and with it he has brought us here."

Cheers arose for Peter, but the boy stood upon his tiptoes and whispered in the Elf King's ear.

The king motioned for silence and then said, "The boy has just told me that it is the cat who actually found the Golden Horn. Somehow he knew about its hiding place. He scratched up the floor of the cave until he found it."

"The cat! the cat! hurrah for the cat!" cried the elves.

"What is cat's name?" asked the King.

"Homer, Your Majesty," replied Grandmother Hollyberry. "He has always been a good cat."

"Let us have Homer up here, so that he can be properly honored," said Elfin.

But Homer, who was suddenly quite overwhelmed with shyness, was slinking away to find a hiding place. One of the elves spotted him, however, and swooped him up. He was passed from hand to hand, until he found himself on the rock with the King. Elfin picked him up and looked deeply into his eyes.

"You have been a hero today, Homer," said the King. "All the people of the Great Forest owe their rescue to you."

Homer felt very much embarrassed from so much praise, yet at the same time so warm and happy and proud inside that he purred.

"Now we must set about the task of freeing the little folk," said Elfin. "Already the gnomes have probably been warned by Klutter and Klatter, but they will not be able to escape. Our magic is stronger than theirs, for we use it only to do good.

"First, we must destroy the Web. That can be accomplished easily enough by spraying it well with the Elixir of Good Spirits. The Elixir is harmless to the good and innocent, but it will dissolve anything evil that it touches. Thus it should serve quite well to free the dwarfs, the deer, and Santa. You, Prince Elfire, shall be in charge of that operation. Gather your elves together. See that they are well supplied with the Elixir, and go in search of the entrapped dwarfs."

Prince Elfire saluted smartly.

"We shall carry out your orders at once, dear Elfin."

"Now we must find the gnomes and King Klutch. We must also determine what is to be done with them. They can never again be allowed to engage in such evil conspiracies against their neighbors," declared the King.

"The Gnome King has planned a banquet to celebrate the victory," said Grandmother Hollyberry. "All the gnomes have been invited. By now they may all be assembled in the main cavern of the Gnome Kingdom."

"Good! That will make our task considerably easier," replied Elfin. "Now, my sprites, let us a-wing! Three miles to the northeast lies the entrance to the underground world."

63

"But *we* can't fly," objected Peter.

"Well, we shall have to take care of that first then," said the Elf King with a smile. He made a swift motion with his hands and muttered some incomprehensible words; and there, very firmly attached to Peter's and Amy's and Grandmother Hollyberry's shoulders were sets of thin, irridescent elf-wings.

"Wow!" cried Peter as he wiggled his back and forth. "Can I really fly?"

"Whether you can really fly or not depends entirely on you. But you have been given the *means* to fly," said Prince Elfire. "Try jumping off this low rock and let your wings have their way."

Peter tried and suddenly he was soaring through the air.

"Whoopee! I can do it! I can fly!" He landed on a hemlock bough high above the ground. "Come on up, Amy!"

Amy sprang from the boulder and her wings carried her aloft.

"Look at me, Peter! Watch me! Watch me!" she cried.

"Come up here," called her brother.

In a moment she was standing beside him on the limb. A cheer went up from the elves.

"You are now one of us!" cried Prince Elfire. "You have helped us to overcome evil with good."

Even Grandmother Hollyberry and Homer had wings. Homer was especially eager to try his. He had always secretly envied birds, who could soar about on the air currents and rise so swiftly and gracefully from the ground, when the best he could do was to scramble up a tree. He flapped his wings and up he went to a branch near the children. Balancing dizzily on the limb, he looked down at the ground far below. Suddenly his old fear of height returned. He half flew and half tumbled down. Crashing through the branches, he landed at Grandmother Hollyberry's feet. She laughed and picked him up in her arms. She understood his problem.

"I do not believe that it is Homer's nature to fly, Your Majesty," she said. "If you do not object, I shall just carry him."

King Elfin laughed and patted Homer's head.

"We all have wings, but we do not all know how to use them. Now let us be off. The sun is in its zenith. Our work lies before us."

64

Then rising into the air, the entire throng of elves soared above the treetops of the Great Forest. A flood of music such as Amy and Peter had never heard before poured from their lips. The golden tones rang through the Forest with such bewitching beauty that the little forest creatures came to the doors of their various abodes to listen. They watched in amazement as the elves skimmed over the treetops like green birds — but *such* birds as nothing in the Forest could remember ever having seen or heard before.

Peter and Amy held hands and flew along with the others.

"What do you suppose Mother and Daddy will say when we tell them about all *this*?" asked Amy.

"*If* we ever get home again," said Peter.

"Oh, Peter! We *must* get home somehow. It's nearly Christmas. Think how worried everyone must be."

"Yes," replied Peter almost reluctantly. "We'll have to get home by Christmas. As soon as this is over, we'll ask the Elf King to help us. Maybe we can even *fly* home."

In little more than an hour they arrived at the entrance to the tunnel which led directly to the Gnome Kingdom. They all marched through the narrow, twisting passageway in single file until they were halted by the rock wall. King Elfin motioned for everyone to stand back several yards. Then he made a swift gesture and the rock exploded into a fine dust which filled the air for several minutes and caused everyone in the tunnel to cough and sneeze. As it gradually settled to the ground, there before them lay the unguarded Kingdom of the Gnomes.

The elves poured into this enormous cavern and once again formed a line of march. Ten abreast, they proceeded toward the royal palace. Since the gnomes were already assembled inside the royal banquet hall, the elves were virtually unopposed. When they reached the entrance to the palace they pushed aside the two guards and entered. The gnome guards tried to strike the elves with their swords and pickaxes, but the elves were protected by an invisible shield from which the gnomes' weapons simply bounced back. The gnome guards set up a fearful howl and scattered in terror.

Straight to the banquet hall the elves marched. Surely enough, all the gnomes of the kingdom were assembled. Seated around hundreds of round tables, they were partaking of the fine food that was being served to them by King Klutch's servants. King Klutch himself was just raising the royal goblet to his lips to drink the victory toast, and all the gnomes had glasses in their hands when the elves burst into the room.

"Surrender!" cried Duke Elflute. "Surrender to his majesty, King Elfin, Royal Ruler of the Elves, Defender of the Great Forest, and Eternal Guardian of the Innocent!"

"What!" roared Klutch. "What does this mean? To arms, gnomes! To arms! Attack!"

The startled gnomes, however, discovered that they were unable to move from their chairs. Some mysterious elf magic had securely fastened their feet to the floor. The elves began to laugh, and their laughter tinkled like music through the banquet hall. The gnomes covered their ears, for the sound of happy laughter always made them feel ill. King Elfin approached King Klutch.

"We have been summoned to the Great Forest, King Klutch," began Elfin, "to rescue Santa Claus, together with his dwarfs and reindeer, whom you have trapped in the web that you purchased from the Black Widows."

"Lies! All lies! You have been grossly misinformed, Elfin," said the wily Gnome King. "We have merely brought them here as guests to the banquet which we are holding in celebration of Christmas."

"Why are they not here with the others, then?"

"They are coming later. The *real* banquet is being held tonight. This is merely an extra party — just for *my* people."

At that moment Prince Elfire rushed into the hall. He heard the last words of Klutch.

"They are not here, King Elfin," he cried, "because we have found them all imprisoned in the net in Sulphur Cavern. The air in there is so foul that they can scarcely breathe, and they are choking and gasping for breath."

"Dissolve the net at once and free them," commanded Elfin. "Let the dwarfs and deer return to North Pole, but bring Santa

66

Claus and his councilors here, so that we may collaborate on a plan of punishment for this monstrous deed."

The gnomes began to howl in terror, and King Klutch turned purple with rage. He seized the royal goblet and hurled it at the Elf King; but Elfin merely raised his hand, and the goblet halted in its flight, turned, and flew back to its former place on the banquet table. Elf laughter rippled through the cave. Klutch scowled. Perhaps, he decided, discretion would be the better part of valor right now. He tried to run, but like his subjects, his feet were stuck to the floor. There was nothing to be done but sit down on his royal throne at the head of the table and await developments.

Prince Elfire soon returned with Santa Claus, Clever, and the other councilors. He informed the Elf King that the dwarfs were free and were already marching happily up the mountain to their homes at North Pole. The deer, too, were once more romping in the forest, grateful to be free of the net and the caves and to be back in their beloved woodland.

When Elfin saw that so much had already been accomplished, he sent Duke Elflute and a contingent of a dozen elves on a secret mission.

"Go to the home of the Black Widows. Seize them and bring them here at once," he ordered.

Then the head banquet table was cleared of food and eating utensils and converted into a conference table. Santa Claus and King Elfin sat down side by side. Santa's ten councilors were seated at his left, while to the right of King Elfin sat the members of his Advisory Committee of Seven. Across the table from them sat the scowling Klutch. The other gnomes were closely guarded by their captors, as the sprites at the table began conferring on their captives' fates.

Suddenly into the quiet banquet hall through a secret door burst Klutter and Klatter. They had trotted as fast as they could through the South Tunnel, but it had taken them considerably longer to reach the Gnome Kingdom on foot than it had taken the elves to come by wing.

When they saw the elves guarding the captive gnomes, they tried to duck back into the tunnel, but they were quickly seized and fastened to the floor with elf magic.

67

He ventured to look over the edge, and again the fear swept over him.

Chapter 12
Conclusion

"**N**OW, KRIS KRINGLE," BEGAN THE ELF KING, "we have the unpleasant duty of deciding the fate of these misguided creatures."

The Gnome King scowled darkly, but dared not speak.

"I suggest," continued Elfin, "that we turn them loose in Sulphur Cavern, where they intended keeping you, and seal them there forever, after stripping them all of their magical powers, of course."

The Gnome King groaned.

"That is a harsh sentence, Your Majesty," objected Santa. "Please let me explain, dear Elfin, what I believe to be the cause of all this trouble. For years the gnomes have literally enslaved themselves. They work for twelve hours or longer every day. Their work is hard, uncomfortable, and often dangerous. They mine the underworld for gems and ore. Sometimes rocks fall on them, crushing them. Occasionally they are trapped by cave-ins. The gnomes who refine the precious metals work by fiery furnaces.

"All this is done for King Klutch, who is the wealthiest ruler in the world, although even he does not know how to enjoy his treasure. The gnomes, most of whom are exceedingly rich, never rest from their labors, since they are extremely greedy. They rarely come to the earth's surface to enjoy the beauties of Nature and to take a vacation. They don't know how to love and enjoy their own children, but put them to work at the ages of six or seven. They don't know how to relax or play. They love little but wealth and work.

"Since they have experienced so little love and pleasure in their own lives, the steps they took that led to our kidnapping and enslavement were quite easy for them to justify in their warped and twisted minds."

"Santa Claus, you are too generous and understanding for your own good," objected Prince Elfire.

"Not so, not so," replied Santa. "Whatever we do, we must bring about a permanent change in the gnomes. Otherwise, Fear will forever dwell in the Great Forest to haunt us like some evil spirit."

"He is right," said Prince Elfsleeves. "What do you propose, dear Santa?"

"I should think that we might draw up a Constitution for the gnomes. Let us depose Klutch, whom we shall probably never be able to reform, and allow the gnomes to hold an open election.

"We must give them a new code and see that it is carried out. They should work no longer than six or eight hours a day. They should also be encouraged to leave the caverns for several weeks each year and spend the time in some pleasant place on the earth's surface. Let us give them some musical instruments and teach them how to sing."

"They are tone-deaf, Santa," objected Clever.

"That's probably because they have never heard anything better than their own cacophony. The dwarfs and I will visit them each Christmas until gradually they will come to know and to keep the Spirit of Christmas in their own hearts and lives."

"That proposal of yours doesn't sound much like punishment," mused King Elfin. "However, you may be right. I shall agree to your terms on one condition."

"What is that?" inquired Santa.

"That we sentence the gnomes to work for six months in the Sulphur Caverns where they were planning to keep you and your dwarfs forever. They must be made to experience themselves the fate that they had planned for you."

When the gnomes heard this, they began to howl, so that it was all the elves could do to quiet them down.

"Very well," agreed Santa. "That may be a good deterrent to future mischief. Oh, and one more thing. Let us have King Klutch donate some of his treasure to establish a shelter for lost or homeless cats."

"What!" roared Klutch. "A cat shelter?" He turned white with rage. "Thieves!" he shrieked. "Thieves! I won't do it!"

70

"Take him away," said King Elfin. "He may begin serving his six-month sentence at once. We agree to accept the Santa Plan. Let it all be done as Santa Claus has proposed."

The gnomes both howled and cheered. The idea of being freed from the tyranny of King Klutch, along with lighter work and vacations above ground, softened the six-month sentence and gave them good cause for rejoicing.

At that moment Duke Elflute and his company of elves arrived with the Black Widows. Even though they were now captives, they were terrifying to behold. King Elfin regarded them in silence for some time and then arose to speak.

"The Black Widows can never be punished or reformed effectively. If they are allowed freedom as they now exist, they will pose a permanent threat to us all. I shall therefore, with your approval, perform a transformation. Never again will they be able to weave a magic web to trap anything larger than insects. I shall never be able to destroy either their poison or their sting, however, so they will to some extent forever remain a threat."

With everyone's approval, he tossed some white powder at the Black Widows. There was a pouf, and the Widows were gone.

"What happened?" asked Peter.

Grandmother Hollyberry pointed to a dozen spiders crawling away in all directions.

"Be careful!" she cautioned. "Don't let them sting you!"

But at least for the time being, the Black Widows had no thoughts of stinging. They desired only to escape forever from the caverns and the dwarfs' wrath. They disappeared as quickly as possible into some cracks in the wall.

"Now as for Klutter and Klatter —" continued Santa.

"What about *them*?" asked the Elf King.

"They are an especially bad pair — two rascals to leave the children and Grandmother Hollyberry tied up in a cold, dark cave."

Everyone nodded in agreement.

"I should like to keep them for awhile at North Pole. They can work as stable grooms for the reindeer, under strict supervision, of course."

71

"Agreed," said Elfin, "but Santa, you must keep a watchful eye on them until you have succeeded in transforming them with your powers of love and kindness."

"I promise to do all that," agreed Santa.

"Now we must hang the Golden Horn again on a limb of Lothra, the Great Oak." The Elf King motioned to Duke Elfleet to take care of this task. "And that should resolve all the problems," he added with a smile at Peter and Amy.

"Your Majesty," Peter ventured to speak out in spite of his shyness in such splendid company, "do you think there is any way you could send us home for Christmas?"

"You wish to go home?" Elfin inquired.

"Mother and Daddy are probably worried frantic," explained Amy. "And besides, we miss them."

"I'm sure of all that," agreed Elfin. "How long have you been in the Great Forest?"

The children hesitated. So much had happened that it seemed like weeks.

"About four days," Grandmother Hollyberry spoke up for them.

"Sending you home is not an easy matter," explained Elfin.

"Maybe we could fly home," suggested Amy, wiggling her wings.

"No. If you were to attempt to fly into the other dimension, you would run into the barrier which separates us and injure yourselves. I cannot send you back in a golden bubble, for only natural-born elves can travel in them from one dimension to another.

"You have become an elf; but if you return home, you will once again become a mortal and lose your elf wings forever."

"You mean we won't be able to fly?" asked Peter, who was reluctant to part with his new acquisition.

King Elfin shook his head. The children looked at one another.

"Maybe we should stay," ventured Peter hesitantly.

"I want to go home, but I still want to be an elf and fly," cried Amy.

"Perhaps we should all go back to North Pole," suggested Santa, "and look in at your parents on my special television screen."

"That is a capital suggestion, Santa," agreed Elfin.

"As you know, today is Christmas Eve, and tonight my dwarfs and I must enter the other world to bring the Spirit of Christmas to mortals. Let us see what your family is doing, little ones. Then if you wish to remain elves, you will be welcome to stay forever, either here with Grandmother or me in the Great Forest or in the Kingdom of the Elves."

"Then we shall leave you to your work, Santa," and King Elfin arose with his advisors. "We must return home. The Golden Horn is safe on the branch of Lothra. Blow it if ever you need us again."

"Good-bye," said Peter. "Whatever happens, we'll never forget you and your elves."

The Elf King took Peter's hand.

"If you return to the world of mortals, remember that, although you may lose your wings, you are forever more an elf in spirit. And you, too." He bent over and kissed Amy's forehead. "Perhaps we shall meet again some day."

Rondo had been led in and Santa mounted upon the huge horse's back. He motioned for the children to climb up too, but they preferred to use their elf wings to fly to the top of the mountain. It was extremely difficult to say good-bye to the elves, for one of the aspects of goodness is a magnetism that attracts everything to it. The farewells were eventually completed, however, and the elves flew off toward their own land, while Santa, the children, and Grandmother Hollyberry, with Homer in her arms, turned toward North Pole. The dwarf guards, along with several of the councilors, remained to carry out the project of reforming the gnomes.

"Do you know, Peter," said Amy as brother and sister skimmed over the treetops, "I'm beginning to feel very, very tired."

"No wonder! We never even got to bed last night. I'm starved, too. It's been a whole day since we ate anything."

By the time they had all gathered at North Pole, however, they discovered that the dwarfs, who had arrived earlier, had prepared a sumptuous repast. Dwarfs are famous for their culinary skills. They spared neither effort nor cost to make this celebration of their rescue an event to be long remembered in the Great Forest.

Amy and Peter were seated at the head table with Santa and Grandmother Hollyberry. Homer was given a place of honor next to Santa. Mistress Mousie, King Dock, Princess Ittypoo, and the Red Bird were all present. Food was also set out for all the little forest creatures to enjoy.

Their plates were filled with delicacies the children had never before seen. But the best part was the dessert — heaping bowls of snow cream topped with elfberries. A napkin was tucked into Homer's collar and he was served his favorite dish — chicken à la sardine with a goblet of golden cream. He was happy to be rid of his wings, for he found them uncomfortable; so King Elfin had removed them.

Everyone ate and drank his fill amidst the music of Christmas carols played and sung by the dwarf children. Blossom and Bud patted Homer shyly. They had heard how he had saved them and the other dwarfs by digging up the Golden Horn. In fact, everyone was talking about nothing but Peter, Amy, Grandmother Hollyberry, and Homer — especially Homer. The recovery of the long-lost Horn was like receiving a special Christmas present.

At last everyone had eaten and drunk his fill. Santa rose to address the merrymakers:

"It is seven o'clock. The night is clear and calm. In two more hours we must embark upon our annual mission. Everything is in readiness. Even now the reindeer are being harnessed to my sleigh and the gifts loaded aboard. Let us give thanks to our four friends."

A great cheering went up from the crowd.

"But let us clearly understand that in spite of all they did, there was another Hand that guided them. Let us never forget that."

Murmurs of approval filled the banquet hall.

"Now we must say good-night. Go to your cottages and sleep well. When you awaken it will be Christmas morning."

At that instant bells began to chime. Their joyous notes rang out on the clear night air, rippling down the mountain and floating out over the Great Forest below.

"Homer and I must be getting back to the Gingerbread Inn," said Grandmother Hollyberry. "If you children decide not to return home, you are welcome to live with us forever in the Great Forest."

"Rondo will carry you both safely to the Inn door, Grandmother," said Santa.

"Thank you, Grandmother, for everything. Amy and I will miss you and Homer very much —" Peter's eyes filled with tears in spite of his best efforts not to cry. Amy threw her arms around Grandmother Hollyberry and Homer both and sobbed aloud at the thought of parting from her new friends.

"Come, come, now," said Santa. "Let's turn on the TV and look in on your parents."

He led them into a small, cozy room. One entire wall was a gigantic TV screen. He switched on the dial and a picture soon appeared.

"Look! It's Daddy — in our living room," cried Amy.

"He's trimming our Christmas tree," said Peter, as he stared in fascination at the image.

"And there's Mother — and Grandmother, too, in the big chair. But — but — they're crying!" Amy's voice trailed off.

"Do you know why they're crying, Amy?" asked Grandmother Hollyberry gently.

The children were silent for a moment.

"Be — because of us?" asked Amy.

"Because they think they have lost you forever," explained Grandmother Hollyberry. "After all, you disappeared without a trace. The police have searched for you. They suppose you have been kidnapped."

"Well, good grief!" cried Peter. "We'll have to get home!" He swallowed the lump in his throat. Amy began to cry again.

"Well, if you really want to return, we'd better get started right away. I won't have room for you in the sleigh because of all the toys, but you may ride on Donder's and Blitzen's backs if you promise to hold on tightly."

They stepped outside to the stable yard. The sleigh was loaded and waiting for its driver. The deer were pawing the snow, impatient to be off.

A full moon made the landscape as bright as day. A dozen or so dwarfs stood around to watch Santa embark upon his annual mission. The children kissed Grandmother and Homer goodbye, not without sorrow at parting.

"If you ever return," said Grandmother, her own eyes filling with tears, "be sure to come back to the Gingerbread Inn."

"We will, Grandmother! We will!" cried the children. But before anyone could say another word, Santa had cracked his long whip, and the eager reindeer plunged forward. Up, up and away they flew. They passed over Troll Valley and the mountain ridge and the Great Forest. Below them they saw the Gingerbread Inn, silent and dark in the moonlit valley. Then they burst into a dense fog and could see nothing at all.

After what seemed like hours, they emerged from the mist and there below them were roads and yards and cottages.

"Look! There's our house!" cried Peter, pointing downward.

"Then we had better land here in the school yard and let you off," said Santa; and in a second the sleigh was on the ground.

"Thank you, Santa! Thank you for bringing us home!" cried Amy.

"Go straight to your house now. I must awa-a-ay . . . ." Already the sleigh was in the air. "Merry Christmas" — his voice trailed off into the night sky along with the jingling of his sleigh bells.

Peter and Amy caught hands and ran down the dark street. Turning the corner they ran without stopping for breath until they reached their own front door. Peter turned the knob, and the door opened.

"We're back!" he shouted.

"Mother! Daddy! Grandma! We're home!" cried Amy.

"The children are here! The children are here!" shouted their father, clasping the boy and girl in his arms. Mother and

Grandma were rushing into the room, and then everyone was embracing them.

"Where on earth have you been? Everyone in the town has been searching for you! Where did you come from?"

"We've been nowhere on earth," replied Amy truthfully.

"We've been to the Great Forest," explained Peter.

"Yes, we took you picnicking to Chester Woods. That's where we lost you."

"Not Chester Woods, Mother," corrected Peter, " — the *Great* Forest. It's in another dimension."

"We got lost and we were hunting for you," said Amy, "but we slipped down a hill on some slippery pine needles and there we were — in the Great Forest! We found the Gingerbread Inn and Grandmother Hollyberry and Homer."

"You see," Peter took up the story, "there were these gnomes who were planning to kidnap Santa and the dwarfs; but *we* found the Golden Horn —"

"Homer actually found the Horn," corrected his sister.

"But *I* blew it. And all the elves came in golden bubbles, and they gave us wings like theirs, so we could fly, too." Peter suddenly felt his shoulders. "My wings — they're gone! So are yours, Amy."

Peter paused for breath. The grown-ups just stared at one another.

"They're delirious from fever and exposure," said Grandma.

"It sounds as if you've been dreaming," suggested Mother. "Have you been in the woods all this time? Did the searchers find you? Who brought you home?"

"Santa," said Amy. "Actually we've seen the Kingdom of the Gnomes and North Pole, too. We came home on Donder's and Blitzen's backs. We came back because we missed you, and we saw you on Santa's great big TV screen, and you were crying."

"We saw Dad trimming the tree," said Peter. "And anyway, if we *were* dreaming, we both certainly wouldn't have had the same dream, would we?"

Amy nodded, and laying her head on her father's shoulder, she sighed, "It's been such a *wonderful* adventure! Such a *wonderful,*

wonderful adventure! Just think! Tomorrow will be Christmas Day! And now we know what Christmas is *really* all about, don't we Peter?"

"A real fairy prince!" cried Amy, clapping her hands.

About the Author

Betty Stewart Behringer *is a prize-winning poet whose work has been published in anthologies and literary journals. She is a native Baltimorean who grew up in a northwest suburb. She graduated from Western High School, Towson State Teachers College, and Johns Hopkins University. She taught English for twenty years in Baltimore. The Gingerbread Inn is her first published story book for children.*

CHP

What the critics had to say about

THE GINGERBREAD INN

"It is the kind of book that can easily become a classic tale."

— OCALA STAR BANNER
Ocala, Florida

"Defending the existence of Santa with some good will, peace, love, and a little democracy, the tale is inspiring to those of us who have forgotten what it's like to wonder if there really is one."

— THE DAILY WHALE
Rehoboth Beach, Delaware

". . . a delightfully fascinating children's book."

— THE ASCENSION LIGHT
Towson, Maryland

"Young reader titles squirm around and vanish: visible are . . . (and) THE GINGERBREAD INN by Betty Stewart Behringer."

— THE BALTIMORE SUN
Baltimore, Maryland

"What a lovely Christmas story! I thoroughly enjoyed how you developed your characters, Peter and Amy . . . and how you created suspense for the reader by depicting the universal theme of good versus evil."

— School Librarian